Looking for LOVE

FINDING GOD'S TRUE PURPOSES IN LOVE AND MARRIAGE

JOANNE GILCHRIST

malcolm down
PUBLISHING

21 20 19 18 17 16 7 6 5 4 3 2 1

First published 2017 by Malcolm Down Publishing Ltd.
www.malcolmdown.co.uk

British Library Cataloguing in Publication Data
A catalogue record for this book is available from the British Library.

ISBN 978-1-910786-63-5

Cover design by Esther Kotecha
Cover image painting: 'Twinkling City' by Zaoming Wu, used by permission.

Printed in the UK

CONTENTS

Endorsements

'As a pastor I've read many books and resources for the purpose of helping people win in their relationships. Joanne's book so clearly presents God's heart for love, relationships and marriage with honesty, humour and great application of God's word.

Looking for Love is therefore a must-read for each young person and every parent wanting to help their kids on the journey we all are on. I hope my daughters read this book one day and gain from Joanne's story.'
Pastor Amy de Vetter, Lead Pastor, Elim North Whangarei, New Zealand

'Reading *Looking For Love* is like meeting a wise friend for a relaxed cup of coffee. One of those encounters that leaves you with a fresh perspective on life. With the perfect balance of honest personal experience, inspiring practical advice and encouraging biblical truth. Joanne invites young women to draw closer to the "perfect one" who alone can satisfy our deepest heart's desires.'
Eileen Barrett, 26, former children's worker at St Thomas Church/ STC Sheffield

'Whether you are considering a relationship, are in one or not, this book encourages you and gives opportunity to search your heart, to understand what it truly desires and find what will ultimately complete your life: relationship with the Father through Jesus Christ. It contains many real life stories and examples that will relate to your story, offering advice and wisdom as you progress through the reflection questions at the end of the chapter. This book will encourage you, make you laugh and help you on the journey of your heart to wholeness.'
Tina Mann, 34, Interior Designer, Solo Artist and Worship Leader at Ivy Church Manchester, UK

'This is a fantastic book, easy to read and refreshingly honest. Joanne understands the struggles and disappointments of looking for love but she has also learnt first-hand that God's ways are best and that His love is greater than any other. Through Joanne's story this book will help you to think about where you are looking for love, encourage you to trust God with your love life and remind you of God's wonderful love for you.'
Hannah Mugenyi, 28, Youth Worker with Lovewise for six years, now freelance graphic designer for Love2Last, UK

'I loved the book! It answered questions that I never even thought of asking. God helped me to understand that I'm not alone and I realised that others face the same issues. Most of all, reading this book brought me closer to my heavenly Father, learning more about His love for me.'
Beth Keers, 19, Student at Cliff College and Children's Worker Intern at the Parish Church of Saint John the Baptist, Owlerton.

'Buy it. Go for it. It's really good. I found *Looking for Love* really challenging. It made me think about what it means to look for love, who am I looking to for love and who am I placing my happiness in. The questions at the end of each chapter were really good and helped me think through what I'd read.'
Becca Howe, 28, Children's Worker & PA, The Oakes Holiday Centre, UK

'This book is a must read for those who are looking for love, but who have questions about the healthiest way of doing this. Joanne speaks from a new level of understanding for those who are dealing with the complex issue of pursuing a deep and personal relationship with Christ and finding a partner. Coming from a personal understanding of the Father's heart for his children, Joanne gives a clear insight into the do's and don't's of dating in a Christian world. The book explores the normal longings of the human heart, giving insight into how Christ wants to be sufficient

for all our emotional needs. From this strong basis of a relationship with our Saviour, the reader is able to make decisions on how to pursue the romantic love that God intended for their lives.'
Sharn Johnson, 37, secondary school English teacher and teacher at Love2Last

'The big thing I got from the book was how reading what Joanne had been through solidified what I was learning in my own life. Particularly about not putting relationships and marriage on a massive pedestal and putting a lot of weight and pressure on some guy to be your ideal. For me it was good to read how our value is not in whether we are in a relationship – our value is in God and the fact that we are children of God and how much He loves us. That was really helpful to read back to myself. The final chapter was my favourite! I loved how it didn't end talking about marriage, but focusing on Jesus and our relationship with God as being of number one importance.'
Fiona Houghton, 19, student of Medicine at Nottingham University

'I found this book really helpful, thinking about marriage and relationships and what I am looking for in a relationship. It made me think, "Why do I want a relationship and who I am seeking to please?" It was really encouraging the way that it pointed me back to God and how I need to be satisfied in Him and how actually He is the only one who can satisfy me more than any relationship. Chapter four was a great reminder of marriage not being the result of human failure or a moral institution, but it is intimately and completely related to Christ and the Church. It's so good to get a sense of the bigger picture of marriage.'
Rebecca Mangles, 19, student at Nottingham University

'This book really surprised me – there were bits in each chapter that really got me. One of them was that you don't need a husband to feel God's love. If you have one, it's a blessing, it's not an achievement. Another amazing thing I discovered was that, like

in a marriage, God actually wants to have a really deep, intimate relationship with me, and it's interesting to ask – do I want that? Or do I want to ignore the best love there is and the purpose God has for my life? And another thing I liked was that getting ready for marriage isn't just about getting excited, but it's also about leaving things behind that could ruin a marriage. And it's easier to do that while you're single than while you're married.'
Dóri Budavári, 24, Hungary

'I really loved the language describing God's love. It made it so tangible and exciting.'
Erica Greaves, 29, Sheffield

'*Looking For Love* is a great book for those that have been single a short time, or for those of us that have been single for years. Joanne has a fun, personal and friendly approach in her writing and you feel like she is talking directly to you, which I loved about this book. Joanne's story is honest and challenging – she's not afraid to admit her own weaknesses – yet through it she shows us how Christ can take our brokenness and truly turn it around. She understands the difficulty in waiting, yet spurs us on to believe that with Christ at the centre, we will be blessed in the long run, whether single or married. It was great to hear not only Joanne's story, but the stories of different women who have found themselves in the single department of life. As a result, you get the feeling that to be single is to be part of a community and that you are not alone. This is so key when much of the Church is focused on family life. When you feel at a loss that you don't have your own family, Joanne reminds us that we are part of the family of God. I especially loved the fact that Joanne leaves space at the end of each chapter for reflection and prayer. This book would make a fantastic resource for friends who want to discuss and grapple with their singleness together, or for someone who wants to work through their thoughts alone.'
Katy Hailes, 32, Ivy Church Kids Team Leader, Manchester UK

Introduction

My name is Joanne Gilchrist and I have a story of the faithfulness of God. From a child of four to a woman of thirty-four, God has taken me on a journey of discovery that continues to unfold even today. I never went through a dramatic period of teenage rebellion involving drugs, sex and rock 'n' roll, but Jesus still saved me. I've been to church my whole life, invited Jesus into my heart when I was four years old and began life as a missionary at eighteen. Yet for all that, I needed saving. Without Jesus I would still be looking for love. Not just looking, desperately searching. Whether I was married or single, I would still be looking for love.

Why? Because of a deep, unfulfilled desire in the chasms of my soul to be accepted and loved.

This book is for those of us who have a deep desire to love and be loved, but who have believed at some point that this desire cannot be filled by God. Perhaps you believe a lover, committed to you through marriage, is the answer? I won't be irreverent or belittle your feelings or say they don't matter, because they are deep and real and vital. I want to honour those feelings, but I also want to bring them into the open and allow the light and truth of Jesus to shine on them so that we don't have to live in darkness, loneliness or discontent.

I want to look at the purpose for which we were made and the purpose for marriage, and compare them to your needs and desires. I want to look at some of the challenges young women face today as we look for love and try so desperately to do it right while seeing so many examples of doing it wrong. I want to give you a fresh perspective – to lift up your eyes – to help you focus on how God sees you, how God sees marriage, and help you find the way to fulfilling the deepest, deepest desires of your precious heart. Let's begin our journey.

Joanne.

Part One: Looking Around: The Search for Fulfilment

Chapter One
Looking Back

Let him kiss me with the kisses of his mouth –
For your love is better than wine.
(Song of Solomon 1:2)

I grew up desperate for a boyfriend. I remember being thirteen and crying for no reason every Saturday night, believing that the sadness in my soul would go away if only I had someone I could call my own – someone to cuddle me on a Saturday night as we watched a movie; someone to hold my hand in youth group or smile at me when I was sad; someone who would look into my eyes, see the real me and tell me all the beautiful things about myself that I longed to hear – perhaps then I would feel complete and whole and happy.

But I also had a desire to do it the right way. I have been a Christian from the moment I prayed my first prayer inviting Jesus into my heart at four years old, sitting on my mum and dad's bed. From then on I wanted to follow God and live life the right way – His way. The problem was, I didn't know what the right way looked like. I was a bit of a flirt – all that desperation had to go somewhere, I suppose – and the attention I got made me feel good for a while, and occasionally I got a boyfriend out of it too. I received an award once in youth group for being 'The Biggest Flirt' – perhaps that was their way of trying to persuade me to tone it down.

So I grew up. Somewhere between fifteen and seventeen I upgraded the term 'boyfriend' to 'husband'. As a teenager I took on board the lessons I was taught about not wasting time searching for boyfriends who would be here today and gone tomorrow, and instead to hold out for a husband. I don't think that lesson had the effect my youth leaders intended, though – instead of calling off my search I just aimed a bit higher: 'OK, so I'm not to look for a boyfriend. I'll look for a husband instead.'

So now I'm about seventeen; still desperate for that love and affection, but determined not to look for it in the wrong places. Every cute Christian guy who crossed my path was in trouble because he was now the target of my ambitions, whether he knew it or not. If he happened to be friendly, I immediately mistook this for true love and spent many a night either imagining the rest of our lives together or wondering why he hadn't asked me to marry him – oops – I mean, why he hadn't asked me to go out with him yet.

Once I hit university I was on a mission. My first goal was to earn a degree, my second was to get engaged. I didn't waste any time getting started on my goals. During Freshers' Week, I sought out the Christian Union (CU) table and was given the details of the first social. The moment I arrived I was on a man hunt. I sought out the best-looking guy in the place and made sure he left with my phone number. The poor guy didn't know what had hit him! After a week or so I asked him out and he was so polite that he said yes and then invited five other people to make it super-clear 'we are just friends'. First attempt failed. OK, who's next? The next guy had the unfortunate traits of being friendly and kind. It was unfortunate for him because all it took was one honest act of kindness on his part and I practically stalked him for about two years, apparently oblivious to the total lack of interest from him. Undeterred, I continued my hunt – I mean, my search – till I had alienated all the boys in the Christian Union. One by one, I managed to make every eligible boy in university a little bit afraid of me. Looking back, the desperation must have been obvious.

APPARENTLY BEING DESPERATE IS NOT THE NUMBER ONE QUALITY A GUY LOOKS FOR IN A GIRLFRIEND.

With this kind of looking for love, I pretty much met three types of guys.

First were the truly honest, lovely, friendly, wonderful young men of God who would one day make fine husbands. However, they were clever and discerning enough to run a mile, or at the very least keep me at a careful arm's length, never looking me in the eye for too long in case I mistook that look for an unspoken intent to propose someday (I mean, unbroken eye contact – that must mean true love, right?).

Secondly there were the less 'gentlemanly' types who weren't concerned with saving themselves for marriage and would assume if I was flirty then I was easy and up for a bit of naughty business. Now, let me make this clear, I wasn't looking for a fling, I was looking for the real thing – a husband. So while these kind of guys were tempting (really tempting!), they were no good for me.

Thirdly, there were the 'nice guys' who weren't very discerning and were pretty insecure too. They loved the attention I gave them and thought I must be 'The One' for them – usually because I was 'The Only One' who had flirted with them all year. They didn't realise I flirted with every bloke because I didn't actually know how to stop.

So the first type would have been great catches, but they weren't biting; the second type would have loved a bite (and a little more besides!), and the third type who were desperate to be caught would have soon realised they'd bitten off more than they could chew.

In those single years I prayed for a man. I spent hours dreaming about a man. I had a recurring dream about a man I believed I was destined to meet some day. I wrote lists about my perfect man and I prayed for my future husband's well-being. I even believed, once, that I heard God tell me the man I was going to end up with and held onto that secret hope for a while. I had wanted this for so long – ever since I was five years old, skipping around the playground singing about a boy till I drove him so crazy he let me sit near his coat while he played football (just to shut me up, probably). In sixth form, I was described by a girlfriend as a 'walking hormone' and at the time took it for a compliment. Oh dear! How horribly unattractive I must have been – in my attitude and behaviour, that is.

Then, one day, I was flipping through my diary and I was sickened – utterly sickened – by the sheer number of boys' names in it. I had imagined myself in love with each of them – a different one every month!

I KNEW SOMETHING WAS HORRIBLY WRONG.

Something had to change, and yet I seemed powerless to change it. For all my efforts, the one thing I believed would change it was a husband. And that was the one thing I couldn't seem to manufacture, persuade or manipulate into being.

Thank God, actually! Looking back now, if I had met my husband while in that state I would have ruined the relationship before it had really begun, because I had no idea what I was looking for while I was desperately looking for love. My perspective was completely and utterly messed up.

Hope in desperation

Perhaps you are not as desperate as I was. Perhaps you're reading this thinking, 'I'm not that bad!' But, even if you are, I have good news – there is hope for you. God changed me. He changed me from the inside out. It wasn't instant, but it was miraculous and believe me, I'm not using that word lightly. God did a miracle work in my life that was a gift to me during those single years and a gift to my husband when I finally met him. It wasn't the result of one revelation or even one great book, but a process of change that took a little time and a lot of trusting God. He saved me. God saved me from a messed-up future of desperately looking for love while never finding it and instead, He showed me the way to love. Perhaps as I share my story, God will show you what you need too.

YOU WON'T FIND A GUIDEBOOK TO MEETING MEN IN THESE PAGES, BUT I HOPE YOU WILL OPEN YOUR HEART TO ALLOW GOD TO TRANSFORM YOU INTO THE WOMAN OF GOD YOU WERE DESIGNED TO BE...

...A woman who can embrace both singleness and relationships with all the blessings, trials and gifts that each stage has to offer. So take a deep breath as we plunge into a journey that will lead us through the deepest chasms of your heart and soul to find The Heart that beats for you.

From a caterpillar to a butterfly

My transformation began while I was at university. It started with the realisation that I was not actually very happy. I remember looking in the mirror one day and realising that when I sang those songs in church – the ones that say 'Lord, You're all I need' – I didn't mean it. I believed that I also needed a man – not just any man, but a husband – to be happy, fulfilled, content, complete. I didn't know if I was right or wrong to say such a thing. At the time, I was just trying to be honest.

It is OK to be honest with God, even if our thoughts and feelings are not what we think God would want to hear. In fact, the safest place to vent all your thoughts and feelings (no matter how unpleasant they are) is in prayer to Almighty God, whose arms are big enough to embrace you and love you even while you are beating on His chest in anguish or fury, like a child having a tantrum in their mother's loving arms.

How do I know this? Because the psalms in the Bible are full of emotions that aren't always what a 'good' Christian ought to be feeling, but they are prayers offered up to God anyway. God acknowledges these prayers – He put them in Bible! – and He acknowledges yours too. Why? Because He knows our weaknesses as well as our strengths. Psalm 103 says: 'He knows our frame; He remembers that we are dust' right after saying 'As the heavens are high above the earth, So great is His mercy toward those who fear Him.'

David, the writer of Psalm 103, cried out in desperation to God again and again and again, and what he said and sang weren't always the wholesome, positive or uplifting songs we turn into modern-day worship songs. They were real and gritty prayers of deep failing and feeling, even if that feeling was a rotten one. Yet God still loved David. David was a man after God's own heart (Acts 13:22) not because he always got it right but because, no matter what, he always turned to the Lord. In good times and in bad, in desperate need and in celebration he always, eventually, came back to God and poured his heart out to Him.

Get Real With God

Do you recognise yourself in these pages at all? Which parts, specifically?

What would your ideal romantic relationship look like?

Do you believe God's love is enough for you?

Do you find it easy to be honest with God?

If there is something you want to tell God, can I encourage you to take some time and do so?

Chapter Two
Pulling Back the Blinds

My beloved is like a gazelle or a young stag.
Behold, he stands behind our wall;
He is looking through the windows,
Gazing through the lattice.
(Song of Solomon 2:9)

It was a conversation that changed my life. Student night at Jumping Jacks, the cheesy nightclub underneath the empty IMAX on Bournemouth's waterfront found me with my Christian Union friends getting a sugar high on Pepsi for a pound a pint, while Chesney Hawkes screeched that he was the one and only and we all joined in. I was dancing in a sea of leery-eyed uni students who were desperate for a snog and grew less and less choosy as the night wore on. Our little group looked out for each other; on the outside I was laughing and dancing and enjoying my friends, but on the inside I still craved more – more love, more affection, more adoration. It was a constant craving that environments like nightclubs promised and yet abysmally failed to give. Like an addict returning to the source of pain I danced and danced, laughed and flirted in the vain hope that one of these young Christian men would answer my heart's cry, fulfil my dreams and rescue me from my loneliness. But the more I looked for love, the bigger the empty space inside me felt.

I had been challenged on my flirtatiousness before. Youth leaders especially tried to get me to change my behaviour, but I insisted I was not flirting. I would say I was only being friendly and it wasn't my fault if the guy got the wrong impression and thought I fancied him.

This time was different. Perhaps the Lord had prepared me,

perhaps it was the gentleness and respect with which my friend spoke or the respect I had for him. Perhaps I was just ready to finally listen. But the challenge of my friend Jamie's words was clear and I owe him a debt of love forever:

'Joanne, you're an awesome person. We've known each other for nearly a year now and I see a lot of great qualities and potential in you.'

Oh my goodness, is he going to ask me out?

'But Jo, there is one area in your life that needs to change if you are ever going to fulfil that potential.'

No. He's not.

'I think you know what I'm talking about... It's the way you act around guys. It's not good. The desperation you give off – most of the guys in the CU are terrified of you. They're afraid that if they are friendly to you, you'll start fancying them, so they stay away. It's not the real you, Joanne. I can see the real you and this flirty, desperate person is not it.'

I can't remember much else about that conversation, but I do remember this part:

'We're setting up small groups soon in houses and dorms, and I know you want to lead one of them, but can we trust you?'

Ummm... Yes?

'Let's say a guy joins your group, a new Christian. Would you be most interested in helping him with his walk with Jesus...'

Yes... of course I would...

'...or would you be more interested in trying to flirt with him?'

There it was. With one tug my friend had pulled back a curtain that I didn't even know was there. He saw right through my phoney façade to the centre of my real problem. He saw past my happy, flirty charade to the desperation behind it. He hadn't run away and he hadn't misinterpreted it. He saw me and cared for me enough to make me see what was so obvious to everyone else.

When an addict wants to recover, the first step[1] is recognising that there is a problem. In a way, I was addicted to flirting! Or rather, it was the attention I received when flirting that I was addicted to.

THAT CONVERSATION IN THE NIGHTCLUB MADE ME FINALLY REALISE THAT I HAD A PROBLEM. AND NO, BEING SINGLE WAS NOT THE PROBLEM!

It was something much deeper than that and it was affecting my relationship with God, my friendships, my leadership potential and any hope of a healthy relationship with the kind of guy I actually wanted.

As we continued to talk in that noisy nightclub, the bass speakers couldn't drown out the word that was beating in my heart that night: *accepted*. I just wanted to be accepted. Deep, deep, deep down somewhere. Maybe the word for other people is different, but I know there is a word that describes not the pain but the desire; the deep, deep desire that no human remedy can even come close to fulfilling. I was a bottomless well that needed an eternal source of love to fill it and never stop filling it.

You see, my problem was not my behaviour. My desperate flirting with every guy I met was merely a symptom of my real problem. My problem was not my Christian community, either – they simply provided the environment for the problem to rear its ugly head. The reason this conversation was so pivotal was because it finally exposed the real problem – God wanted to address a deeper need, one no mortal man could fill. My problem was a desire to be accepted. I hid it behind a charade of extroverted, flirtatious behaviour, keeping the real me hidden away in case I revealed it, only to be rejected. Although I didn't know this at the time, when people rejected flirty Jo, it didn't matter so much because that was never the real me anyway. Jamie ignited a spark of desire in my heart – the desire to find the real me. The real me God made me to be. The true me that God believed I could be. If I'm really honest, I'm still on that journey!

Our emotional needs

There are deep needs within us – the need to give and receive love, the need to be accepted, the need to belong to something greater than ourselves, the need to feel secure, and the need for intimacy are just a few. Emotional needs are as real as physical needs such as food and water, and everyone born since the beginning of time has them.

Researchers and psychologists have spent the last century trying to define them, map them out and analyse them.[2] There was one group of psychologists who called their list 'Given Needs' because they are simply there in our DNA, programmed into the genes of every human being, of every age, race and gender.[3]

As Christians we are privileged to understand that there is a creator God in heaven who 'programmed our genes'. The needs He gives us are given for a reason and purpose. That means...

GOD NOT ONLY 'PROGRAMMED' OR DESIGNED THE NEED, BUT HE ALSO PROVIDED THE SOLUTION FOR THOSE NEEDS TO BE MET.

Just as a physical need such as feeling thirsty has the physical solution of water, so our deeper needs have a deeper solution, generously and graciously provided for by God.

God has provided us with communities, families, husbands, parents, children and friends to help meet those needs, but they only meet some of those needs some of the time. These needs run so deep that no human love is deep enough to fulfil them all the time. When you are thirsty and the water in your bottle has run out, you need to go to the place that water came from. For the purest, most refreshing water you need to go to the source – a fresh spring or deep well. Love from other humans is like water from a bottle – it meets the need for a while, but your needs are deeper than one bottle of water, or one other human being, can fulfil.

They are so deep that the way to receive the best, purest, richest, most fulfilling kind of love is to go to the source. That source is God. He is the source of all love on earth and beyond it. Just as all water on earth originates from and flows to the ocean, so all love on earth originally comes from Him, and we can direct our love back to Him like a river runs towards the sea. 'God is love' (1 John 4:8) wrote John, the disciple who frequently referred to himself as 'the one Jesus loved'. He wrote that 2,000 years ago and it is just as true today as it was then. God is not just loving or lovely – *He is Love*. His supply of love never ends, and God is able to fill you up with love today just as He did for His first disciples.

I mentioned before that if I had met my future husband while in the state of desperately looking for love, I would have ruined the relationship. The reason is because my need was greater than one imperfect man's love could ever fulfil. To ask another human being for an unending spring of eternal love to keep you happy and satisfied is to ask for something only God can give. I'm sure my man would have tried his best for a few months, maybe even a few years, but sooner or later, he would be exhausted and drained and have nothing left to give, while my bottomless heart still needed more love. God made the bottomless well in your heart to be constantly and forever filled with His everlasting source of unconditional love.

This is not just a message for the young and single, but if you are privileged enough to receive it while you are still in that place you can enjoy your single years with all the gifts and benefits it has to offer. If or when the time comes to marry, you will be able to enjoy that relationship and everything it has to offer without the disappointment of unmet, unrealistic expectations. It's not your expectations that need to change – your desires and needs are important and God wants them to be fulfilled – but who are you looking for to fulfil them?

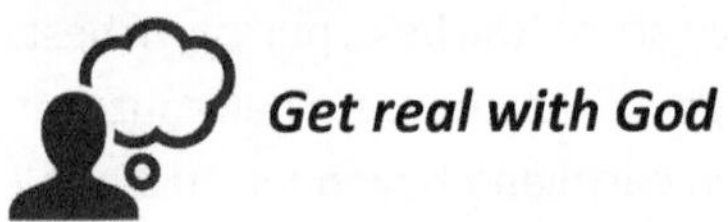

Get real with God

What are you looking for in a relationship?

My word was 'accepted'. Is there a word that describes what you are looking for, deep down? Here's a list from a book called *Top 10 Intimacy Needs*[4] – do any really stand out to you?

Comfort	Acceptance	Love
Affection	Encouragement	Peace
Appreciation	Respect	Attention
Approval	Security	Support

Do you believe God can meet those areas in your life, or have you been looking for someone or something else so meet them? Ask God to show you.

Finally, here's a prayer you might want to pray before we move on:

Father God,
Thank You that You love me and that You want me to know Your love in a more real way than ever before.
Please open my eyes to see myself as you see me.
Amen.

Chapter Three
A Fresh Perspective

Do not be conformed to this world,
but be transformed by the renewing of your mind.
(Romans 12:2)

So the process has begun. We've figured out the problem, but how do we fix it? You have probably already guessed there is no magic potion that will give you your instant happy ever after, but there is an answer and it can be found. The solution involves transformation – like changing from a caterpillar to a butterfly. It takes a little time and there are certain processes that need to take place before the butterfly can emerge with strength to fly.

Part of that process involves a new way of thinking. Romans 12:2 says that if you want to be different to the world around you, you need to 'renew your mind'. This means...

TO LIVE DIFFERENTLY, YOU NEED TO THINK DIFFERENTLY.

And in order to think about yourself and the world the way God does, you need to read God's word: the Bible. In the next few chapters, I'd like to look at what Jesus and the Bible have to say about this relationship known as marriage. Perhaps you aspire to marriage like I did, or perhaps you've gone in the opposite direction and couldn't care less about marriage as long as you are getting your needs met. I don't know. What I do know is that when marriage, the lack of marriage, or the hope of marriage becomes all-consuming to the point where you are dissatisfied with your relationship with God, then something has been distorted somewhere about the role of marriage and the role of Jesus in your life. So let me share with you a few insights God showed me about that mysterious relationship we call marriage.

Marriage is not for ever

Jesus explained that one day (after the resurrection of all believers) there will be no marriage or giving in marriage (Matthew 22:30; Mark 12:25; Luke 20:34–35). Huh? This stopped me in my tracks for a while. No marriage in heaven? So that means that marriage is not eternal. That means that marriage is temporary. Yes, it is a covenant (a promise, a contract) but covenants are only binding till death (Romans 7:2). And death isn't the end – we have a whole eternity still to come afterwards! Marriage is for life, but it's not for eternity.

So if marriage is temporary then it cannot be the ultimate goal or achievement in life. I knew enough of my Bible to know that everything that is temporary will one day be gone and only the unseen, eternal things will remain (2 Corinthians 4:18).[1] I knew to fix my eyes on the eternal, to put my treasure in heaven, not into things on earth (Matthew 6:20);[2] to focus on things that last, things that really matter (Philippians 4:8).[3]

Somehow, in our cultural frenzy of happy ever after fairy-tales, 'How I met The One' sit-coms and 'I love you forever' pop songs crooning in our ears every day, it is easy to miss this simple but utterly life-changing fact: marriage is not forever so it cannot possibly be the ultimate prize a person can achieve in life.

In Philippians 3:12–14 Paul describes his motivation for life. He describes himself as working, running to win the prize, the crowning achievement, the mark of a successful life:

> Not that I have already obtained all this, or have already arrived at my goal, but I press on to take hold of that for which Christ Jesus took hold of me. Brothers and sisters, I do not consider myself yet to have taken hold of it. But one thing I do: forgetting

> what is behind and straining towards what is ahead, I press on towards the goal to win the prize for which God has called me heavenwards in Christ Jesus.
> (The Bible)[4]

Back in university, when I took an honest look at my thoughts and feelings, they went a bit more like this:

> Not that I have already obtained marriage or arrived at my wedding day, but I press on to take hold of a good husband that Christ has chosen for me. Brothers and sisters, I do not consider myself to yet know who that husband is but one thing I do: forgetting all the losers in my past, I press on towards the goal of marriage to win the husband for which God has called me to marry.
> (Not the Bible)

I know I can make light of this in retrospect, but for some of us this is a pretty accurate description of the way our thoughts lead. It sounds funny but it's really very serious.

The wedding is not the end of the story

I don't know for sure, but if you are reading this book perhaps you believe or once believed like me that the wedding is the end of the story – that your wedding day will be the ultimate climax in the story of your life. So many fiction novels, romantic stories, children's and grown-up movies end in a wedding (or at least the couple finally getting together) that it's easy to assume that getting the man or winning the girl is the ultimate prize in life.

Logically, if marriage were the end of the story then after marriage there should follow an eternal bliss. Perfection. The happy ever after we are all waiting for. You'll never be sad or cry or have to say sorry ever again (as one ridiculous line from a popular

1970s love story went).[5]

But after marriage does not come perfection – just ask someone who is married! If marriage was easy, we wouldn't need the thousands of books written or counsellors trained to help married people put the 'happily' back in 'happily ever after'.

Still, when we are single we sometimes hold onto the hope that our future marriage will be different. When we get married it will be perfect because God will provide the perfect man, right? Well, yes and no. Yes, we can trust God to provide a great partner for our lives, but if you think that man will solve your problems, meet your needs, heal your hurts and finally win you the prize of a successful life, then you are putting an unnaturally high expectation onto another human being. You could even say a supernatural expectation, because it will take someone who is more than just a human being to do all that.

Let's say you do get married believing that your husband is the perfect man and you are being promoted to 'married status' due to some level of maturity on your part. When then? What about when the inevitable happens and you realise he isn't perfect and neither are you? Do you give up on the marriage because you obviously picked 'The Wrong One', and your perfect man is still out there? Or do you give up on yourself, thinking you are too flawed to ever have a great marriage?

Or do we make like Romans 12:2 and change our thinking, renew our mind and get a proper perspective on love, life and marriage? Perhaps – and be prepared to have your mind blown here – perhaps, there is something other than marriage that is the goal and something other than a husband that is the prize?

The wedding actually is the end of the story after all

Where in the Bible can we find eternal bliss, perfection, no sadness or suffering, no need for saying sorry because there's no sin? We find it right at the end of the Bible, in Revelation 21:1–5. The apostle John is writing, describing a vision God is showing him:

> Then I saw a new heaven and a new earth, for the old heaven and the old earth had disappeared. And the sea was also gone. And I saw the holy city, the new Jerusalem, coming down from God out of heaven *like a bride beautifully dressed for her husband.* I heard a loud shout from the throne, saying, 'Look, God's home is now among his people! He will live with them, and they will be his people. God himself will be with them. He will wipe every tear from their eyes, and there will be no more death or sorrow or crying or pain. All these things are gone forever.' And the one sitting on the throne said, 'Look, I am making everything new!' And then he said to me, 'Write this down, for what I tell you is trustworthy and true.' (NLT, emphasis mine)

Interestingly enough, a spotless eternity, free from any sin or suffering does actually come with a wedding day after all. But not the wedding day we might have expected. In the story of the world – our story – a wedding does come at the end and we, the Church, are the bride. Eternal bliss is coming. Perfection is coming. The end of suffering and the restoration of every good thing is coming, and it comes on the day that our relationship with God is fully restored to the same level (or perhaps an even higher level) of unbroken intensity as it was in Eden. This 'happily ever after' is not reserved for those who happen to get married during their lifetime here on earth. It is available to everyone who believes in the Son of God, the Saviour and the maker of heaven and earth (John 3:16).

There is a 'happy ever after' coming, but it doesn't start with your earthly wedding day to an earthly husband. It starts the day you give your heart to the bridegroom. Who is that bridegroom? Who is our Saviour, the healer of hearts, the fulfiller of dreams, the one who meets all our needs?

THERE IS ONLY ONE MAN WHO EVER LIVED THAT REACHES THAT CRITERIA AND HIS NAME IS JESUS.

Our love affair with Jesus can start today and continue to develop throughout our lifetime till the day we meet Him face to face.

What I'm really trying to get across is that getting married is not a prize given out by God for those who have done well or achieved success. Neither is it the goal or ultimate achievement in life. Why? Because it is temporary. And the Bible tells us that real things are eternal (2 Corinthians 4:18), including the prize that Paul is running after in Philippians 3.

That leaves us with two questions. Firstly, if marriage is not the goal and a husband is not The Prize, then what is the point of marriage and relationships? Secondly, what in the world is the prize and how in the world do I get it?

A true story: Maarten and Esther's wedding day

The day had finally arrived. It was a rainy February day outside, but inside the modern Dutch sanctuary the church gathered together, rumbling with expectation and anticipation. A nervous man in a morning suit hovered near the front, briefly shaking hands with splendidly dressed friends and distant relations. Around him flitted two or three similarly dressed younger men who seemed to be busy: shifting from one side of the aisle to the other, tweaking chairs, checking notes in pockets, glancing at the clock. The gathered crowd were slowly filing into place, forming row upon row of suppressed, excitable bodies, ready, waiting for the bride. Everyone present knew just how long the bride and groom had waited for and prayed for this day – both the man near the front in his fifties and the coming bride in her early thirties. They had overcome times of testing, endured personal difficulties and persevered through sickness and distance to meet and marry on this glorious, wonderful, happy day. When the bride finally entered, the music began – uplifting, worshipful music, praising the God who had led them there. They held hands as they sang with all their heart to the Faithful One. And the Spirit of the Faithful One responded. His presence filled that room like a rush of mighty wind, uplifting the hearts of every believer and amazing the unbeliever. A thickness, a deepness to His presence could be almost tangibly felt. It was electric.

As the marriage celebrant began to speak to the congregation, he spoke of a greater wedding day to come; one even greater than this one. He described the way Maarten and Esther's engagement was a period of waiting, persevering and overcoming all kinds of trials in order to reach this climactic day. In the same way, the people of God are waiting, persevering and overcoming all kinds of tests and trials, in order to be there, ready and waiting, on a day a zillion times more climatic and more glorious than even this one.

He said, 'It is a wedding day that all believers get to be a part of. It is when Jesus comes back to claim His Bride and present her to His Father, with worshipping angels as their witnesses. It's a day so magnificent that in the Bible it is simply called "The Day".'[6]

The smiling faces, the wonder-filled hearts, after listening to the preacher, continued to witness this earthly marriage with an awareness that as amazing as this experience was, there was an even greater occasion to come. This was merely a dress rehearsal, a blueprint, a shadow of the real thing.

Get real with God

Have you ever believed marriage to be the goal of life, or a husband the prize for a successful life? Why do you think some people (like my younger self) think that?

What do you think is the point of marriage?

Would you like to get married some day? Why?

What do you imagine when you read about the new heaven and earth in Revelation 21? How does it make you feel to read those words? How do you think Jesus feels about it?

Chapter Four
Marriage Under the Microscope

'For this reason a man shall leave his father and mother and be joined to his wife, and the two shall become one flesh.' This is a great mystery, but I speak concerning Christ and the church.
(Ephesians 5:31–32)

When God first dreamed up the whole concept of marriage, what was He thinking? If marriage is not the goal of life or the ultimate prize, what it is the point of it?

If you have been to many weddings or are the kind of hopeless romantic who has watched *Pride and Prejudice* over and over, like I have (1995 Colin Firth version, of course), then you will know the following words off by heart. These are the words that have been spoken at millions of weddings over hundreds of years. They are from the *Book of Common Prayer*[1] and I think they are truly inspired:

> DEARLY beloved, we are gathered together here in the sight of God, and in the face of this congregation, to join together this Man and this Woman in holy Matrimony; which is an honourable estate, instituted of God in the time of man's innocency, signifying unto us the mystical union that is between Christ and his Church; which holy estate Christ adorned and beautified with his presence, and first miracle that he wrought, in Cana of Galilee; and is commended of Saint Paul to be honourable among all men: and therefore is not by any to be enterprised, nor taken in hand, unadvisedly, lightly, or wantonly, to satisfy men's carnal lusts and appetites, like brute beasts that have no understanding; but reverently, discreetly, advisedly, soberly, and in the fear of God; duly considering the causes for which Matrimony was ordained.

Time out for a second. All those long, old-fashioned words basically say that marriage is good and godly. It was God's idea from the very beginning, before sin entered the world. God first described it this way: 'That is why a man leaves his father and mother and is united to his wife, and they become one flesh' (Genesis 2:24, NIV UK 2011). Marriage also helps us understand the relationship between Christ and the Church. The speech then goes on to say that marriage is honourable (Hebrews 13:4) and that Jesus honoured marriage with His first miracle at a wedding (John 2:1–11). Therefore, we should all think of marriage as a serious thing and take our time before committing to it, making sure we really understand what it is all about.

> First, it was ordained for the procreation of children, to be brought up in the fear and nurture of the Lord, and to the praise of his holy Name.
>
> Secondly, it was ordained for a remedy against sin, and to avoid fornication; that such persons as have not the gift of continency might marry, and keep themselves undefiled members of Christ's body.
>
> Thirdly, it was ordained for the mutual society, help, and comfort, that the one ought to have of the other, both in prosperity and adversity. Into which holy estate these two persons present come now to be joined. Therefore if any man can show any just cause, why they may not lawfully be joined together, let him now speak, or else hereafter for ever hold his peace.

To sum up, in twenty-first century language, this is what it says:

Marriage is incredible! God invented it and Jesus blessed it – it says so in the Bible. (marriage is marvellous)

Marriage helps us understand some of the mystery of the relationship between Christ and His Church. (marriage is a metaphor)

God gave us marriage to provide a secure environment for children to grow up where they could learn about the character of God through such relationships as mother and father. (marriage makes family)

God gave us marriage so we could have awesome, guilt-free, pure, holy sex. (marriage makes holy sex)

God gave us marriage so we could have a friend, helper and companion for life. (marriage is a marathon, not a sprint)

1. Marriage is marvellous

Marriage is incredible! God invented it and Jesus blessed it – it says so in the Bible.

When I read that marriage service I think,

'WOW, MARRIAGE REALLY IS AMAZING!'

It is truly incredible, good and godly. It is such a wonderful thing, and it is good to desire it. God really, really does love marriage. He designed it, He honours it, He encourages it and He blesses it. And here's why.

Marriage began in Eden before sin ever entered the world, so it is not the result of human failure. It is not a patch-up job to make us feel better or a moral institution invented by human beings to try to control the masses. No. It is a God-made answer to the God-made need for human companionship.

Man was lonely and woman filled a need that God had created in him. The idea of creating a male and a female occurred in the same moment in God's mind (Genesis 1:26) – woman was not an afterthought or a second attempt! However, physically, God created man first (Genesis 2:7). There may be many reasons why God did this, but I believe one of them was to expose the need in the man for the woman – a companion comparable to him

(Genesis 2:18). He had a specific need, she met it (Genesis 2:23) and the world was perfect.

So in a perfect world, woman completed man. And if the world was still perfect, woman would still complete man. But it's not. In this imperfect world, man and woman do meet some of each other's needs – the needs for human companionship, for family and for sex. But – and this is a big but – in this imperfect broken world, those are no longer our only needs. We still need God.

When humankind sinned for the first time, the relationship between God and humans broke down and another need, a deeper need, was left unfulfilled too. And this is where we get mixed up. As human beings, we are very good at using practically anything in God's creation to mask this deeper need. For some of us, we confuse the simple need for human intimacy with the deeper need for unconditional love and an unshakable identity in a flawless, eternal Father.

2. Marriage is a metaphor

Marriage helps us understand some of the mystery of the relationship between Christ and His Church.

God loves to teach us about Himself.

THE WHOLE BIBLE INVITES US TO DRAW CLOSER TO GOD, TO KNOW GOD BETTER, AND NOT JUST IN AN ABSTRACT WAY BUT A PERSONAL WAY.

The problem is that most spiritual concepts are abstract – forgiveness, covering of sins (atonement), purification of character (sanctification), love, fear of God, righteousness... not only are they long words but very difficult concepts to understand. Even the idea of 'the Church' – millions of people spanning thousands of years, from every nation and people group all united under the leadership of Jesus – was a concept completely hidden from every person and prophet in the Old Testament.[2] It was a mystery, hidden since the beginning of time, hinted at during the life of Jesus and finally birthed after He had gone up to heaven, with the coming of the Holy Spirit.

To help us understand this great mystery of the Church, the Bible gives us several metaphors (it is so mysterious that one is not enough!). The Church is likened to a kingdom with Jesus as King, a body with Jesus as Head, a family with God as Father, a temple with Jesus as the High Priest, an army, an assembly, a workmanship and finally a bride with Jesus as Bridegroom.[3]

Each one of these metaphors is a visible picture designed to teach us about something that is invisible. Marriage all by itself is an incredible, amazing thing and a wedding is a celebration that is the highlight of many people's lives, not just the bride and groom. But as a metaphor it is something even more amazing.

Have you ever seen the French movie *Amélie*? Probably not, it's French. But if you had, you'd remember a scene where Amélie has left blue arrows for her lover to follow so he can find her. The arrows lead to a human statue that is pointing left and upwards. He stares and stares at the statue, trying to understand what it means. Eventually, a little boy approaches and says to the man, in French, 'When a finger is pointing up to the sky, only a fool looks at the finger.' And the man stops staring at the finger and continues his quest, following the direction that the finger points.

So if marriage is a finger... (I know this sounds absurd, stick with me) only a fool stares at marriage and thinks they have reached the end of the treasure hunt and found what they have been looking for. When you read the Bible, you will recognise that marriage is just like that human statue, with a huge, neon, pointing finger stretched towards heaven, screaming: 'There is a greater marriage awaiting us, a greater wedding day still to come.'

A good marriage can do that – it can model Christ and the Church in a way no other relationship does. It can be a light, drawing people towards the Light of the World. Maarten and Esther's wedding day did that – the excitement of the day, the sense of God's presence, the personal story of unity overcoming adversity – all of it was like a blueprint of the real wedding day to come, a taster of eternity, a big, pointing finger drawing our focus towards Jesus.

3. Marriage makes family

God gave us marriage to provide a secure environment for children to grow up where they could learn about the character of God through such relationships as mother and father.

When a man leaves his mother and father and becomes one with his wife, it is the beginning of a new family – or at least, a new branch on the family tree.

Family is at the very heart of everything God does on earth. Adam and Eve were a family. His chosen people, the children of God, the Israelites, were one big family. The Church is likened to a family and God, all by Himself, is a family. What do I mean by that? God created families because He is a family! He is Father, Son and Spirit. When Jesus came to earth He showed us that God is a Father and that if we have faith in Jesus, we have the right to call God *our* Father (John 1:12).

We were created in God's image and likeness, which means we were made to function in groups, communities and families, just like Him.

WE THRIVE WHEN WE KNOW WE ARE LOVED AND NURTURED AND BELONG.

Jesus knew who He was because of His Father. Many people tried to label Jesus – demons called out 'You are the Holy One of God' and yet they were silenced.[4] Crowds of followers tried to make

Him king after He fed the 5,000 but Jesus disappeared[5] because He knew the fickle hearts and opinions of men cannot be trusted.[6] Some called Jesus Elijah,[7] others a prophet or a good teacher.[8] Some recognised Him as Messiah. Yet it was His Father God in heaven who gave Him His true identity: 'My Son, in whom I am well pleased' are the words spoken from heaven twice. The first time they released Jesus into His ministry on earth[9] and the second time they prepared Him for the cross.[10] He was secure in the identity His Father gave Him.

We too get so much of our identity and security and love from our family – we are daughters, sisters, nieces, cousins and often wives and mothers. It's not all we are, of course, but it's a huge part. And how do we make family? A family that reflects the intimacy and commitment and beauty of the Trinity? It begins with two becoming one. It begins with marriage.

4. Marriage makes holy sex

God gave us marriage so we could have awesome, guilt-free, pure, holy sex.

Holy simply means 'set apart'. When you decide to only have sex within God's boundary of marriage, you are setting it apart – you are setting it to one side and saying it is not for whoever, whenever, wherever, but for a specific time (after marriage) and with a specific person (your hubby). You are making it holy.

God commands us to be holy because He is holy (1 Peter 1:16).

SO WHEN YOU GET MARRIED AND HAVE SEX WITH YOUR HUSBAND, YOU ARE BEING HOLY.

Just like God told you to be. Good for you!

Holy sex means no guilt or shame and you have God's permission (and His pleasure) to enjoy it as much as you like. In fact, the Bible even tells you to! It says if you're married, don't stop having sex unless it is for a specific time of fasting and then make sure you carry on having sex again (1 Corinthians 7:5). So when you are married, be a good girl and enjoy plenty of great sex. You can even pray about sex – in fact, I would recommend it because it's a vital part of the relationship. As preparation for marriage you could ask God to help you be a good lover to your husband, or ask Him to help you if you are worried. You can invite God into the bedroom and He is not ashamed to be there because it's holy.

Yes, the waiting bit is difficult and we'll talk about that more later, but when the waiting is over and you're a few months into your marriage, I can promise you, you won't even remember how difficult it was to wait – hopefully you'll be too busy enjoying yourself.

I know talking about sex can be a bit awkward – I am a total English 'prude' so I find it awkward sometimes too. But I want you to know (and this is so important) that when it comes to sex in marriage, there is no shame – it is not shameful or dirty or wrong or taboo. It is holy.

5. Marriage is a marathon, not a sprint

God gave us marriage so we could have a friend, helper and companion for life.

So far, if you're young and single and want to get married, the sex part and the wedding day and the wonderfulness of it all is probably what is uppermost in your mind – totally normal. But there is another side to marriage and that really begins to hit home a few years in: companionship. It sounds boring but if you plan to be married for the rest of your lives, stuff that sounds boring in your twenties might be vital in your fifties, sixties and seventies. Who wouldn't love to celebrate their golden wedding anniversary, after all? But fifty years is a long time. That's not a quick sprint, that's a marathon.

A close friend of mine has run two marathons; one early on in his running career and the other about twelve years later. After the first one, he told his friends to never let him run another one. It was hard work and at times it was agony. Twelve years later, the marathon bug catches him and he signs up again! This time he is more prepared. This time he has read advice from running magazines and invested a lot of time and money in the training and preparation. One trick he learned, for example, was that when he slowed down at the start of the race, he had so much energy later that his overall times improved and he even had energy in reserve to sprint the final half mile, overtaking a few other frustrated – and incredulous – runners!

When we know we are in something for the long haul, it pays to be prepared. It pays to learn from the mistakes of others who are older and wiser, to take advice, to commit to not giving up when the going gets rough. Marriage for fifty years isn't just about sex and a great wedding day. It is so much more lasting than that.

Joyce Meyer writes this in her book *Help Me I'm Married!*:

> The blending of two individuals into one harmonious marriage is a process that takes time. God said that marriage will bring two people together and cause them to become as one flesh... The marriage vows do not supernaturally bring two individuals into perfect harmony. On the contrary, the wedding vows are a promise that they will not give up on each other, in spite of their differences, sickness, and successes, but will commit to waiting on God's plan to work in their lives.[11]

So even though 'two becoming one' is a long process with lots of highs and lows, at the end of the day, point number five is what marriage is really all about. When you're too old for sex (as if!) and your kids have flown the nest, when your friends have all moved away and you're just a 'bum-on-a-pew' in church, there is one person who, if they've kept their promise, should still be there. As Susan Sarendon's character so eloquently puts it in the 2004 movie *Shall We Dance*:

> We need a witness to our lives. There's a billion people on the planet ... I mean, what does any one life really mean? But in a marriage, you're promising to care about everything. The good things, the bad things, the terrible things, the mundane things... all of it, all of the time, every day. You're saying 'Your life will not go unnoticed because I will notice it. Your life will not go unwitnessed because I will be your witness.'

However...

No metaphor is perfect. No marriage is perfect and no family is perfect either, except the one we call Trinity. The fact is, these earthly institutions such as weddings, marriages and families are imperfect. They were not designed that way – they were originally designed at the very beginning of creation, when the world was unbroken. They were designed to perfectly mirror heavenly realities. But the mirror is no longer pure, it is cracked and warped and smoky because of sin. The Bible says that right now our human understanding of these amazing heavenly concepts is incomplete but one day, in the new heaven and earth when there is no more sin, we will see more clearly.

> Now we see things imperfectly, like puzzling reflections in a mirror, but then we will see everything with perfect clarity. All that I know now is partial and incomplete, but then I will know everything completely, just as God now knows me completely. (1 Corinthians 13:12 NLT)

I am not naïve about the reality of marriage today. My parents never had an easy marriage and after thirty-one years of it they divorced. I always knew it wasn't an easy marriage, but I was proud of them for sticking at it and modelling to us the power of God to redeem even a difficult partnership. When they divorced, my first thought was 'but you were supposed to be my role models'. I felt utterly let down.

But then the other day, I told a friend exactly what I've just written and I realised that I do still believe that – I still believe in the redeeming power of God to restore and transform any willing person and any willing couple. The example they gave me has not been lost. Even when it all goes wrong, my faith in God's plan for marriage and everything I have written in this chapter is still very strong.

Sometimes a husband does not love his wife 'as Christ loved the church' (Ephesians 5:25, NLT). Does that mean Christ doesn't love us anymore? No, of course not. But it does mean we might find it harder to understand just how much Christ loves us.

Our experience of family is supposed to help us understand and know God better, but...

WHEN FAMILY DOESN'T WORK OUT THE WAY IT SHOULD, GOD STILL WORKS THE WAY HE SHOULD.

He still loves. He is still faithful, even when we are unfaithful (2 Timothy 2:13). So if your experience of family, mothers or fathers, relationships or marriage has not been a positive one – God is still good. He still loves you and He still promises good for your future if you trust Him.[12] The truth about God never changes[13] – He is always good, always holy, always just and always love. It is just harder to see that when the mirrors God gave to reflect this are dim and mottled by sin.

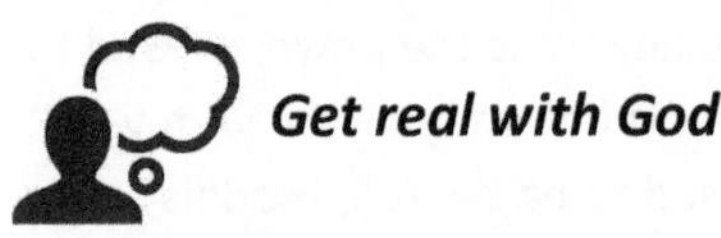

Get real with God

Which of the five aspects of marriage listed in this chapter do you find the most appealing?

What characteristics of God have you seen when you look at a loving, functioning, healthy marriage or family?

What has been your experience of family and marriage? Has it helped you understand God's love for you, or made it harder?

What do you think about the idea of holy sex?

Chapter Five
Marriage is a Mirror

You are all fair, my love,
And there is no spot in you.
(Song of Solomon 4:7)

The last chapter looked at all the highlights of marriage, all the reasons why it is so very, very good. But there is another side to a good marriage which demands a whole chapter all to itself. This truth about marriage wouldn't go on any advert if you were trying to persuade people to buy. In fact, married people like to keep this bit quiet so you only learn it the hard way, when you've been married a few weeks and think to yourself, 'No one told me it would be like this!' It doesn't sound good at first, it sounds horrible, but it is actually very good. In fact, it might even be the whole eternal point of marriage. Really.

Let's look at the Ephesians passage on marriage.

> Husbands, love your wives, just as Christ also loved the church and gave Himself for her, that He might sanctify and cleanse her with the washing of water by the word, that He might present her to Himself a glorious church, not having spot or wrinkle or any such thing, but that she should be holy and without blemish. (Ephesians 5:25–27)

This says that Jesus 'sanctifies' and 'cleanses' us to be his bride. What does that mean? Are we not already forgiven? Didn't God already 'cleanse' us when we first repented and decided to follow Him? Yes, He did. So this bit of the Bible is not talking about our salvation, it is talking about our character. To 'sanctify' is about shaping and improving our characters to become more like Jesus.

Let me explain using a popular analogy from the Bible, which you've probably heard before.

Silver and gold are precious metals dug out of the ground and then 'refined' to separate them from all the other elements that are mingled in when it's dug out. Silver or gold is refined (i.e. purified) by being put into a refiner's fire. A refiner puts the gold into the hottest part of the fire, and guess what happens? All the impurities are raised to the surface. Then the refiner scrapes or brushes off the impurities, leaving what remains all the more pure. He does this more than once and each time the gold becomes more and more pure.

Jesus came to be a refiner's fire to test us and purify us like silver or gold (Malachi 3:2; Zechariah 13:9; 1 Peter 1:7; Job 23:10; Proverbs 17:3; Psalm 66:10–12). When we go through difficult times, when the heat is up and the pressure is on, Jesus allows that heat to raise all the impurities and ugly bits of our lives to the surface, where they can be swept away. A refiner's goal is to make the metal pure. Jesus' goal is to make our characters more pure and our faith more resilient.

How does the refiner know his work is done? When he looks into the surface of the gold and can see his own reflection looking back at him. How does Jesus know His work in our lives is done? When He looks at us and sees Himself – His own character – with His mark upon our foreheads (see Revelation 22:4). This is what He sees on that last day, our wedding day, when heaven and earth are made new. Until then, we are all a work in progress.

There are all kinds of situations Jesus uses as a refiner's fire. And a really, really fun and surprising one (to the newly-wed) is marriage! Why? Why does that passage in Ephesians liken such a wonderful thing as marriage to a purifying fire? Because living in such close community with someone – with anyone or any group of people, in fact – brings out the worst in us. That's why. Think about it. Can you think of any time you have been thrown together with someone, or a group of people, and all sorts of bad attitudes came out?

WHEN THE HEAT IS ON, THE WORST COMES OUT.

Marriage makes us more like Christ

In chapter three, you read the story of my friend Esther's wedding to Maarten. Esther is a beautiful person inside and out. She is a person I look up to because of her faith and character. Whenever there is a problem, Esther is the first person to say 'Let's pray' and you know she will pray for you when she says she will. She has been a nurse and a missionary all her adult life, delivering medical aid to poor and isolated communities over three continents. She is one of the kindest and least selfish people I know.

Yet within six months of her wedding day she said to me: 'I think marriage is very much like a mirror and I've been very disappointed in myself. I think, "Man, I so need the grace of God!" I'm a sinner and I need God's grace and forgiveness and I'm not a bit better than Maarten or anyone else!'

In those few short months of marriage every impurity in her character, the ones she had kept so well hidden from her friends, colleagues and even herself, came rising to the surface in the heat of a committed, lifelong relationship! I'm afraid I laughed when she told me, because it is crazy but true.

You know how you can watch a movie and think it's really funny, till your parents walk in and suddenly you are much more aware of all the dodgy bits? Marriage is like that. You think you are fine until suddenly, someone else is watching you and living with you and you see things in yourself that you didn't see before. Anger, stubbornness, sarcasm, laziness, irritability, passive aggression, moodiness, bad manners, snobbishness, vanity – the list is a long one!

I love the way Pastor Andy Stanley from Northpoint Church in Carolina, USA puts it in his 'Staying In Love' series.[1] He says married couples find that when the honeymoon is over, all this junk in their lives comes out and they tend to blame each other. These attitudes and behaviours were so well hidden before they got married, so newly-weds assume it must be the other person's fault. But those impurities were already in them long before they got married. It's just that their guard is down, they are comfortable being themselves and not as careful with each other as they were when they were dating, and what was once hidden now spills out.

The good news is, Jesus has given us a safe, committed, trusting environment of love where these characteristics can be brought into the open so we can deal with them together: it is called marriage.

Doesn't that sound like fun? I bet no one ever said to you: 'Try marriage. It'll improve your character.' It's not number one on our wish list. It's not even there in the *Book of Common Prayer*! It's certainly not a perk. So perhaps there's no rush to wish our single years away. When or if you meet your man it will be wonderful, but with it comes a refiner's fire and God will know when you are ready to endure it.

Let me continue this topic of marriage with a practical example that will also remind you of one of the perks (in case you are feeling like you never, ever, want to get married after reading this chapter).

Sex and marriage

I remember having a conversation with my best friend at university about men and women and sex. I was thinking about the way we have been created to enjoy sex, and how it is so different between men and women, or so I'd read.

I had found a book tucked away on my parent's bookshelf – I think it was called *The Act of Marriage*.[2] It explained to me something I'd never heard before (and shy girls, prepare yourself – we're going to use the O word!). It said that a man can reach the climax of pleasure in sex (i.e. orgasm – there it is!) very quickly, and when it is over, it is over. For him, it is a short pleasure but very intense. A woman is the complete opposite. She takes a long time to warm up but when she gets there she can feel the climax of pleasure again and again and again before she has had enough. A man wants it short and intense, like a gas flame, a woman wants it slow and long-lasting, like an electric cooker.

This made no sense to me at the time. Why would God create sex in such a way? A way that is so opposite to each other? How are we supposed to both enjoy sex when we clearly require such different methods to do so? Take turns? As a young, single adult, chatting with my best friend while walking the beach in Bournemouth, I could not understand what God was thinking when He deliberately made us that way.

If sex were purely for pleasure, then it wouldn't make sense. If it were a purely mechanical act as a way to produce babies, then it wouldn't make sense either. It only makes sense if sex is about more than pleasure and more than duty. It only makes sense if sex has something to do with becoming more like Christ. Sounds strange? Stay with me.

Remember that book I told you about – *The Act of Marriage*? Well, it had more in it than analogies about gas flames and electric burners. In fact, it was more like a really detailed instruction manual on what to do, how to do it, which bits to touch and for how long, all with one goal in mind: mutual, simultaneous, orgasm. After I read this book I thought, 'Now I know exactly what to do on my wedding night. I just have to follow the instructions in the book.'

Big mistake. Unfortunately for me and my future husband, that book left me with the impression that good sex is a formula and by following the formula, we could get it perfect first time. (I'm afraid I tend to put unrealistically high expectations on myself).

So – spoiler alert – skip ahead to my wedding day and by 10:30pm I can feel a growing nervousness like a knot in my stomach. I had built up this huge expectation that we will follow the manual and have perfect sex first time – all this without communicating it to my poor fiancé.

Needless to say, the best sex of my life was not our first time. I'm not even sure you could call what we did on our wedding night 'sex'. I think it took at least a week just to get the hang of it. And if my expectations had been different, it would have been a fun week! But because of my ridiculous expectations, it was a week of feeling a bit rubbish about myself and wondering if I'd ever get it right.

I wish on our wedding night we had just snuggled up in bed with a hot chocolate and watched a movie, because even that would have been one step further than we'd ever been before. I wish we had taken the pressure off ourselves and just had fun!

What that book didn't communicate to me was that sex is more than a mechanical function to be performed perfectly on a regular basis if you want to be a good wife. And the goal of sex is not mutual orgasm – that's just a bonus!

Sex is about intimacy. Intimacy requires trust and trust requires time, commitment and vulnerability. My perfect plan to 'get it right' first time failed when I realised that we had never actually seen each other naked before. This all by itself was a huge step to take and it took some getting used to – it felt completely bizarre at first. The day after we got married I asked – 'Can we just go and do something normal, like a walk in the park? Something we would usually do? Because we don't usually do this bedroom stuff and I just need some normality!'

Intimacy and good sex did not come immediately in my marriage but odd as it may sound, I am very thankful for that. I am thankful because I plan to be married for a very long time and the best of our sex life was *not over* with the honeymoon. I'm thankful because eleven years into my marriage I am still learning new things about sex and finding deeper levels of intimacy with my husband. I am thankful that we got to learn and practise with each other. Firstly, we had to learn how to do it – that was hilarious! – then we had to learn to trust each other, and after that we had to learn how to talk about it so that we could trust each other more and relax with each other more. Looking back, I think it took me six years to completely relax with my husband! Though I didn't realise it at the time.

And the great thing is that it didn't matter one bit that we didn't get it perfect first time. Our marriage was not over because of it. I know, and I've always known, that he isn't going to leave me if I don't perform well or learn quickly enough. He isn't going to judge me if I starting putting on a little weight. He isn't going to tease me when I feel embarrassed. How do I know that? Because we are married.

WE HAVE MADE A PROMISE AND COMMITMENT TO EACH OTHER, TILL DEATH PARTS US, AND WE DON'T HAVE TO GET EVERYTHING RIGHT FIRST TIME.

These days I am very rarely dissatisfied with my sex life. That book did teach me a few tricks after all! And after eleven years I could tell you some stories that would make your eyes pop out. Sometimes sex is so amazing that I think we've reached perfection and we never need to do it again – but then I remember it's not about performance, but about intimacy.

One amazing phenomenon I've experienced is that some of our most intimate times together have been after hours of honest, open, vulnerable conversation. It was as if the intimacy my husband and I developed in our conversation carried over into the bedroom and it was wonderful. You can't fake that kind of trust and you can't conjure it up just by reading the right book.

Is this making sense? Sex, like many other aspects of marriage, wasn't designed to be a mechanical act of perfection that you can achieve by reading a book. It's not that shallow! To experience it at its best, it requires a relationship of trust, which requires time and commitment. What might a relationship based on trust, time and commitment look like? It's called marriage. The best sex is in marriage.

But let's not forget the pleasure bit, either. Once you've built enough trust to be relaxed and vulnerable with each other, we still have this problem of being made differently – to enjoy sex in different ways. But what if we were generous? What if each partner was more concerned with giving, instead of taking? Romans 12:10 encourages us to 'give preference to one another in [love]' (NASB) – can this can be applied to sex as well as other areas of life? Absolutely! But giving selflessly does not always come easily. In the heat of the moment, we might want to take as much pleasure as possible and then ask afterwards – how was it for you? Great sex takes selflessness and generosity – two trademarks of a refined character.

Generosity, selflessness, honesty, love, patience, kindness, trust, intimacy, commitment, willingness to listen (meekness). All these are ingredients to a good sex life. And above all this – a sense of humour!

Do you recognise that list? Have you seen that somewhere in the Bible before? 'Love, joy, peace, patience, kindness, goodness, faithfulness, gentleness, and self-control' – you find that list in Galatians 5:22–23 (NLT). We call these characteristics 'fruits of the Spirit' because they are the result of trusting God with your life, even when you go through the refiner's fire, to become more like Jesus.

Let's not skip over that last one: self-control. Self-control? In marriage? Why? First of all, it takes self-control to 'forsake all others' and only have sex with your spouse. Secondly, self-control will also be necessary when the other partner doesn't want it or can't. Every marriage experiences times of being apart, or times when one of you is ill, or recovering from having had a baby. Some illnesses or treatments (like IVF, for example) require couples to abstain for long periods of time. Yes, self-control to care for the other person's needs when yours aren't being met is hugely necessary.

More than marriage

This paradox in marriage is just one example of the reality of married life. It is not the only one. Ever heard the term 'opposites attract'? Look closely at couples around you and you'll notice that people don't marry mirror images of themselves. Sometimes extroverts marry introverts, brash loudmouths marry sensitive souls, morning people marry evening people, outdoor lovers marry homemakers, dog lovers marry cat people...

This is not an accident. God made us differently on purpose. Why? So that by living together we can become more like Christ. At first it is a bit of a surprise when the heat is up and you see the scum in your life rising to the surface, but in the end it is an opportunity to deal with it, forgive, humble yourself and say sorry, pray, move on and grow. In fact, it's a survival tool – we have to become more loving and generous or we would kill each other!

One of the best bits of advice someone gave me when I was making a list of qualities to look for in a future husband, was not to look for someone who has all the same qualities as me, but for someone who appreciates those qualities in me. Two people who are the same will soon get bored with each other. It's our differences that we admire and find attractive in the beginning, and it's our differences that present just the right amount of challenge for us to overcome, in order to remain happily married.

Now this is really, really important: the perfect man for you will not be a flawless individual who can do no wrong – no, the perfect man for you will rub you up in just the right amount of wrong way in order to expose your own character flaws that Jesus wants to deal with in your life! But that same man will also love you enough to bear with you, overlook your flaws, forgive you and keep loving you anyway. As the Bible says, 'love covers a multitude of sins' (1 Peter 4:8, NLT). Isn't marriage great?

Finally, let me be very clear – marriage is not the only way to become more like Christ. Singleness itself is a refiner's fire with its own challenges to live a loving and righteous life. Both singleness and marriage are used by God to prepare you to be His bride. My point is this: do not think that by getting married you will escape the refiner's fire. You're just exchanging one fire for another! And both have their challenges but both have their rewards too. The best thing to do is...

ENJOY THE STAGE OF LIFE YOU ARE IN TO THE FULL, BECAUSE YOU NEVER KNOW WHEN IT MAY CHANGE.

Sex before marriage

While we are on the topic of sex and marriage, I would like to address a thought that's been gaining interest in Christian circles lately. That is, that the answer to overcoming the awkwardness when two virgins (or celibates) marry after a long period of abstaining, is to skip the long period of abstaining and start having sex early. The thought is to make it more normal, get rid of unhelpful hindrances right from the start. I cannot agree that this is a solution to intimacy in marriage. In fact, I find it absurd. If you follow Jesus, at some point your lifestyle will clash with the culture we live in. Jesus said so several times (John 16:33; Matthew 5:11; Matthew 10:22). Just because sexual intimacy in marriage takes time doesn't mean you have to start before marriage. It will take time no matter when you start, but it will be even harder to develop true intimacy when there is no commitment, no safe space.

Perhaps we are trying to combine two things instead of choosing one – the cultural way of doing relationships, with God's view of marriage. By this I mean long periods of dating or engagement then immediately expecting movie-sex on our wedding night. Perhaps we think we deserve it as some kind of reward for waiting. Yes, long periods of waiting may mean it will take longer to get used to each other in a new way, but of all the solutions to this problem, sex before marriage is, in my opinion, giving up and giving in. Jesus lists sex before marriage as part of a long list that includes lying, stealing and murder (Matthew 15:18-20).[3] He describes it as one of the things that defiles a human being. So for the Christian, how can sin ever be the answer? Especially if one key aspect of marriage is to become more like Christ. There must be a better solution – in fact, there are probably many, many better solutions before we have to go so far as to accept sex before marriage as the new norm for the Christian way of life.

Perhaps, instead, we simply accept that we might not have perfect, hot movie-sex first time and that there will be some awkwardness and unfamiliarity to overcome. Time, good communication, advice from married friends, realistic expectations, a pace you are both comfortable with, a sense of humour, kindness, patience and love for each other will all help with that. Then the journey of discovery with each other, in the safe, loving committed space of marriage will hopefully bring strength and joy to your marriage. Look at that! I've almost written the entire list of the fruits of the Spirit from Galatians 5 again. Of course! It really is simple. When there is a problem there are two ways to overcome it: sin or the Spirit. I choose the Holy Spirit every time.

Alternatively, we can follow the Bible's advice: go ahead, stop procrastinating and marry. Then have sex (1 Corinthians 7:9). You might not think it is the ideal but it's an option. In fact, I had dinner only a few weeks ago with a couple who had a quiet, civil ceremony early in their relationship and later – perhaps when the wedding venue they wanted became available! – had the big white wedding her family expected of her. For them this was the ideal solution to balancing their desire to live together plus their financial needs with everyone else's expectations. True story: when I was engaged, my mother suggested that if we couldn't handle abstinence before marriage then we could get married early and she would support us. Because we lived on opposite sides of the country, she offered us her house as a halfway place where we could meet up every weekend till it became possible to live together. Can you imagine? Living apart but using your parents' place as a convenient halfway-house for sex? Thanks, Mum! It was nice to know we had options.

Who do you trust with your love life?

It is one thing to know what the Bible says about sex but when the hormones are raging, everyone else you know is doing it or talking about it, and marriage is a long way off – I know it's not that easy. One thing that makes life easier is when you have made a firm commitment in your own heart and mind to wait for marriage. A half-hearted commitment will crumble under pressure. What do you need to make that commitment in your own heart and head?

Perhaps a few statistics will help? Studies have shown that the more promiscuous a female is, the less oxytocin (love hormone) is released into her bloodstream during sex.[4] That means that the more people a woman has sex with, the less fun sex becomes for her – less meaningful, less emotional, less satisfying and less of a buzz (all the things oxytocin does for you). Or perhaps it would help to hear that if you have sex before marriage you're more likely to have an unhappy marriage[5] and more likely to get divorced.[6]

But ultimately, the question of when to have sex, and who to have sex with, comes down to trust. Who do you trust? Do you trust your teenage friend? Your favourite celebrity? The author of a book? Or do you trust God, the maker and creator of human beings, marriage and sex?

Everyone has a standard for when to have sex. Most people would agree that sex should only occur when it is mutually consensual: that is a standard. Others say it should only be when you are in love. Our laws also say it should only be with human beings over a certain age who are not close family members. These are all standards. We all have a standard, based on what we believe and who we follow. We follow who we trust. We may follow the law (I hope you do!), we may follow the majority of current culture, or we may follow God.

God's standard is a very clear one – no fuzzy edges – it is precise to the day you make your vows to each other: 'That is why a man leaves his father and mother and is united to his wife, and they become one flesh' (Genesis 2:24, NIV UK 2011).

Sex within the lifelong commitment of marriage is His standard because that is what sex was made for. Anything outside that has a lot of fancy words – adultery, fornication,[7] debauchery,[8] lasciviousness,[9] lewdness, lust... but in a nutshell they are all sexual sins that Jesus died for.[10]

Yes, no one is perfect and we will all sin, mess up and make mistakes – we'll talk more about that in the next chapter. But a disciple of Christ makes every effort to stop sinning and keep following. When you make a conscious choice to deliberately and knowingly sin on a regular basis, you have to ask yourself – am I really following Jesus? Or am I going in a different direction? We follow who we trust.

Can you trust Jesus with your sex life?

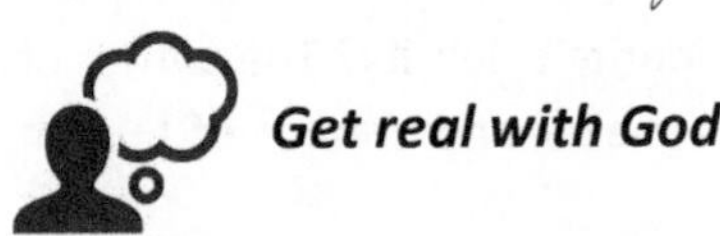

Get real with God

Read Psalm 66:10–12.[11] Would you say you have had experiences that were like a refiner's fire? What were they?

Notice especially verse 12: where are we being led to?

When people say 'you have to work at a marriage', what do you think they mean, in light of what you've read in this chapter?

Read Romans 5:1–5 and Galatians 5:22–23. What qualities is God looking for in us?

We've talked a lot about sex in this chapter, but it has mostly been in the context of marriage – holy sex, remember? Why is it important to talk about holy sex in a positive way?

Can you trust Jesus with your sex life?

Chapter Six
Finding 'The Wrong One'

Catch us the foxes,
The little foxes that spoil the vines ...
(Song of Solomon 2:15)

Jesus once did a miracle by feeding over 5,000 people with just a few fish sandwiches (Mark 6:30–44). You would think after seeing that, Jesus's disciples would have complete faith in Him to be their provider and deliverer. But that very night, their faith was tested (verses 47–50) and it became apparent that they had completely missed the point of the lesson (verse 52; see also Matthew 16:9). The Bible says they did not understand the miracle of feeding the 5,000 because they had hardened their hearts. They had seen the miracle with their eyes but it had not sunk down from their head to their hearts. They still acted like scared unbelievers when the circumstances were against them.

You see, there is a little bit of a delay between learning something and really knowing something. There are different kinds of knowledge.[1] There's the kind you know in your head and the kind you really know in your heart. When we talk about knowledge, we usually talk about head knowledge – we have tests to examine the information we memorise in our heads, and we like to figure things out logically and conclusively with physical evidence before we allow our heart to really believe it.

Then there is the kind of knowledge that is hard to define. We know it without knowing how we know it. It's not information we store in our head, but a truth: an awareness that we feel throughout our entire being. It's knowledge of the heart, like knowing you are in love.

In our culture, we value head knowledge and try to accumulate as much of it as possible, but it's our heart knowledge that actually influences the way we live or act. Plenty of people have been told Jesus is the Son of God and that He loves them so much that He died for them – they know it like they know $e=mc^2$ – but it doesn't change their behaviour because they don't really understand what it means or how it's relevant to their lives. It's not till head knowledge becomes heart knowledge (something we know and believe with all our being, not just our head) that our lifestyle, character and decisions begin to reflect this truth.

So how does something change from head knowledge to heart knowledge? How do you go from just believing something to living it? According to Romans 5:3–4 and James 1:2–4 – after we have been tested.[2] And that makes sense, right? When you learn something at school, it's usually because sooner or later, there's a test.

My test

By the time I was nineteen years old I thought I had learned something about looking for love, but so far I had only learned it in my head. Even though I realised I had a problem and began to make some changes in my life, I had not yet learned to look to Jesus to fulfil my desires. Instead, I thought I should come to terms with being single and let that become my goal.

SO I SILENCED MY NEEDS AND DESIRES AND RELEGATED THEM TO A BACK ROOM TO BE QUIET WHILE I GOT ON WITH MY LIFE.

They had been subdued but not yet fulfilled, so it didn't take much to reawaken them with double force when a wolf in sheep's clothing walked into my life (actually, he kind of danced his way in).

This wolf in particular was funny and gorgeous and he liked me. He was not a Christian, but he was interested in God and we talked about my faith a lot in the beginning. At one point he even had a spiritual experience[3] when he visited my home church but, like my dear friend Jamie had predicted, I got in the way. Instead of being a friend, I allowed my own desire for more to ruin any chance I had of leading him to Jesus.

It was a relationship I never thought I'd find myself in. It was as if the Lord allowed me to experience what I thought I wanted since I insisted so much on having it. (Yes, the Lord sometimes does this – just like the prodigal son story in Luke 15:11–32, but He is also ready and waiting with arms of love when we turn back).

This guy truly was everything I thought I wanted in a man. Good-looking, charming, funny, liked the same music as me etc, etc. But he was exactly the opposite of what I needed. Like I said, he was not a Christian. He said he respected me but he could never properly look me in the eyes. That should have been a clue. He was 'The Wrong One', but I thought maybe I could turn him into the right one. He had the potential.

Another dear friend of mine who once found herself in a similar relationship told me: 'He has all the right qualities, they're just all mixed up and in the wrong places so he comes across as very selfish and self-centred.' Oh, the excuses we women make when we meet 'The Wrong One'!

The concept of Jesus being the one who fills my bottomless heart was one I was actually fighting against. And it took a heartbreak – no, a heart shatter – to realise it. That is exactly how this relationship ended – with an incredibly painful heart shatter.

I remember the wonderful date in the park when this guy told me he loved me. And I remember the text I got the next day, taking it back. I remember trying to break up with him and I remember him begging me for 'just one more day together'. I remember telling him I wasn't going to have sex with him, and I remember him thinking that meant 'everything but'. I remember the phone call when he told me he'd had sex with someone else. I remember finding out he had a double life – no wonder he never let me meet his friends. I remember crying all through the night from a place so deep I thought I'd never stop. I remember trying to cry silently so my parents wouldn't hear and find out what an idiot I'd been to trust this guy. I remember the songs I listened to the next day and I remember hardly knowing how to pray, I felt so ashamed. We may not have had sex, but I'd done enough to make me feel shame. To make me feel sick that I'd wasted my beauty on a man so, so, so unworthy.

I gave this guy my heart and he played with it. He didn't treasure or cherish it, but he bounced it around and threw it up in the air then dropped it and gave it back to me in a messy pile of pain.

That poor heart that should never have been given to him in the first place was utterly shattered and left in pieces. Oh-so-humbly I gathered up the pieces and turned to Jesus and asked if there was anything He could do with it. And oh-so-gently, He pieced it back together. It wasn't quick but it was complete.

I know it was complete because even though I remember all those things I just told you, I can no longer feel the pain. At the time, I would listen to songs and watch movies that resonated with my pain and made me feel it over and over, because pain was all I had left to connect me to this man I thought I was in love with. It was less than a year afterwards that I remember listening to the same songs and watching the same movies, but incredibly, the pain was gone. Not just subdued, lessened or faded into memory – but gone, eradicated, removed, healed.

Muscles have memory – they remember pain, and my heart remembered for a while.

BUT JESUS DID NOT JUST DO A PATCH-UP JOB ON MY HEART – HE MADE IT NEW AGAIN.

He restored it completely. There's not even a scar. (Sometimes, in His mercy, He allows a scar to be left to remind us of how He rescued us so we don't get proud or make the same mistake again, but this was not one of those times).

I forgave the man who broke my heart, humbled myself before God, repented of having given it to someone so unworthy in the first place and bit by bit, my heart was healed completely.

I hope you learn some incredible truths through this book, but I also know that second-hand head knowledge is not enough to live by. We live by faith, in grace and truth, and these things are the result of trials and temptations. When you find yourself going through your own difficulties, or if you are struggling to walk with Jesus and are being pulled away by temptations around you, remember these two things:

Firstly, Jesus is praying for you. He is rooting for you, hoping and desiring with all His being that you will overcome. I know this because He said so to Simon Peter, recorded in Luke 22:31–32, and the same is true for you and me. Read what Jesus says to Simon Peter:

> And the Lord said, 'Simon, Simon! Indeed, Satan has asked for you, that he may sift you as wheat. But I have prayed for you, that your faith should not fail; and when you have returned to Me, strengthen your brethren.'

Look at what Jesus is saying. He's not denying the test – He's predicting it! (He does this at other times too).[4] And Jesus is committed to praying for Peter throughout the test, and most of all He is praying for his faith not to fail. Everything else may go out the window – your reputation, your purity, even your relationship but, as long as your faith remains, you will have the strength and the courage and the determination to return to Jesus and help others. Notice that Jesus says 'when you have returned to Me', which means He knows Peter will fail but He also knows that Peter will return. The failure is not the end of the story, and when you have returned you will be able to do one very important and wonderful thing, and that is to strengthen others around you. I pray that in your test you will not fail, but even if you do, that you will return to Jesus, the 'author and perfecter'[5] of your faith, and continue to walk in the good works He has prepared for you (like it says in Ephesians 2:10).

The second thing to remember is that Jesus is the healer of hearts. If you don't think you did too well in your time of testing, Jesus specialises in redeeming – that means He accepts the offer of a horrid, broken, messy, ugly situation and promises to transform it into something good, beautiful, whole and glorious. Didn't He form the world out of an unformed mass (Genesis 1:2)? Didn't He transform the abuse Joseph received from his brothers into a situation that saved the lives of more than one nation (Genesis 50:20)? Doesn't He promise that to all who trust Him, follow Him and give their messy circumstances to Him, that He will bring good from them (Romans 8:28)? Yes, yes and yes.

There is no broken heart that He cannot mend.

JESUS IS AN EXPERT AT TURNING A BAD SITUATION INTO A GLORIOUS ONE.

In fact, He is committed to doing that very thing until the day He returns to begin anew with the whole of heaven and earth (Isaiah 65:17; 66:2, 2 Peter 3:13, Revelation 21:1).

Let me finish with one final thought – you don't have to fail the test. You might just pass it instead. If you find yourself in a situation where the temptation is too strong, where you find yourself giving your heart or your body to someone who does not love you, does not cherish you, does not value you as highly as Jesus values you, then there is only one thing to do – run. Leg it. Flee. 1 Corinthians 6:18 says 'Flee sexual immorality'! 2 Timothy 2:22 says: 'Flee ... youthful lusts [and] pursue righteousness, faith, love, peace with those who call on the Lord out of a pure heart.'

Don't try to resist it – that's a different Bible verse (James 4:7) for a different situation. Just get out of there. When Joseph was being seduced by his boss' wife, he didn't try to reason with her or 'stand firm' and let her paw her hands all over him – he ran away so fast that he left his coat behind in her clutches (Genesis 39:12).

Remember that one question: 'Who do you trust with your love life?' In the moment of temptation, when your hormones are racing, your heart's beating, your head is swimming and you're fighting an inner battle between 'This makes my body feel really good' and 'This is so wrong', don't hang around. When you do, the very next thing you will feel is confusion – a well-known tactic of the enemy (James 3:16). Confusion will lower your defences and make you forget who you are and what you are worth.

Let me remind you how much you are worth, dear one. What makes a painting so valuable? Not the ink and canvas, not even the time spent on it by the artist, but how much someone else is willing to pay for it. That is how valuable it is.

Jesus was willing to pay for you with His life. The glory of heaven considered you so valuable that He died for you – that is how much you are worth. Anyone who does not recognise your value and your worth is, quite simply, 'The Wrong One'.

Get real with God

Have you ever pushed so hard for your own way that you got it, even though it wasn't good for you? (In other words, have you ever learned something the hard way?)

Do you know what it feels like to have your heart broken?

Have you experienced the power of God to mend a broken heart? Would you like to?

If you need to, pray this prayer with me:

Father God,
I'm sorry for going my own way instead of Yours. Please forgive me. Please take this heart of mine and do what You will with it. Please help me to go Your way from now on.
Let me be wholly Yours once more.
Amen.

Part Two:

Looking Up: Changing Perspective

Chapter Seven
The Promise

My beloved is mine and I am his.
(Song of Solomon 2:16)

So far in my story, after facing my need and submitting to God to change me, I faced a test and failed more spectacularly than I had ever failed before. Amazingly, in that brokenness I was in a place to be made new. Like an emerging pot on the Potter's wheel (Jeremiah 18:1–10), I wasn't finished yet, but my heart was like soft clay – open and willing and available to be changed and moulded into the model that God pictured in His mind when He made me.

I knew now what not to do.

I knew that chasing one guy after another didn't work. I knew that being flirty didn't work. I knew that picking one I wanted and trying to change him into the one I needed didn't work. So what in the world was I supposed to do?

At university, I asked a few church leaders that question: 'Can we please get someone to come and tell us what we should do? Because I already know what I shouldn't do, and as long as I'm trying really hard not to do that, I can guarantee that's exactly what I will do.'

There are some books out there that focus on what not to do. I remember when a Christian friend at university read a Christian book about 'how far is too far' and called me to ask my opinion on how far she could go with her boyfriend. After reading about all these physical sexual acts she shouldn't be allowed to do, she got so horny she went right out and did them. Duh.

It is one of those intriguingly bizarre bits of human psychology that what we aim for is what we hit.[1] I did my gap year in the north of Belgium where we rode bikes absolutely everywhere (it was flat so it was easy) and I discovered an incredible phenomenon. When I wanted to mount the kerb from the road I would look at the steepest part and think, 'Don't hit that.' Then I hit it. Every time. After many sore bottom bumps I tried something different. I decided instead to look at the shallowest part of the kerb and, deliberately ignoring every other part, I fixed my eyes on the shallow bit and it was like magic – I hit it. I hadn't done anything differently other than change my focus.

I'm not the first one to stumble on this profound insight. Cricketers are told to aim to hit the ball towards the gap between the fielders rather than look at the fielder and hit it straight to them. The dieter who focuses on the food she *should* eat will end up thinner than the one focusing on the food she shouldn't.

This principle can be applied to almost any area of life. It can be applied to relationships. If you spend most of your free time thinking about what you should not be doing, sooner or later you will find yourself doing it.

Looking up

So I think we need to focus less on the problem and all the wrong ways we have that do not solve it. We need to change our focus.

I'm going to ask you to try something, if you dare. Try tilting your head all the way back – so far back that you can practically feel it resting on the back of your spine. Have a go and then come back to reading the book.

In the Bible, the phrase 'lift up your eyes' can be found several times. Sometimes it is the Lord speaking through a prophet or Jesus Himself speaking. It is an attention-grabbing cry for the people of God to change their focus either to see what God sees, or to look up towards God for help and for rescue in difficult times. In Psalm 121 the opening lines are a statement, saying: I will not focus on the trouble around me but will focus on the rescuer instead.

> I will lift up my eyes to the hills –
> From whence comes my help?
> My help comes from the LORD
> who made heaven and earth.[2]

If God is up and all the distractions of this world are around you, what can you see when you look directly up? What you can't see is what is around you. When you look up towards God and focus on Him and Him alone, all the other distractions around you become less important. So instead of looking around us for the answer, I'm going to spend the rest of this book focusing on what is up. My hope is, just like the old hymn says, that as you 'Turn your eyes upon Jesus, look full in his wonderful face, ... the things of earth will grow strangely dim, in the light of his mercy and grace'.[3]

The Promise

One day, when my broken heart was nearly mended, I sat in my room and wrote in my diary something profound. I didn't know it was profound at the time, but when I looked back at it later, I realised it was.

I IMAGINED JESUS STANDING IN FRONT OF ME AND ASKED HIM WHAT HE MIGHT WANT TO SAY TO ME IN THAT MOMENT.

And I began to write. At the time I thought it was my own thoughts, but later I realised that God was speaking to me very clearly. I knew because these thoughts were so very far from my own natural thoughts that were full of self-doubt and uncertainty about the future. These thoughts were powerful and didn't change no matter how I felt. This is what I wrote:

God is saying 'I need a testimony from you. Through your weakness, My strength will prove perfect. My glory will shine through you because of this, but I am not finished yet. Be patient oh My darling, darling child. I will take care of you. What harm could possibly come to you while My hand is over you? What protection can a man give that I can't? I want my testimony of you so I can say – this is My child, see how she trusts in Me!

'You have the capacity to give and receive love. A huge capacity! Imagine what fun I could have filling it! If you would only let Me. Do you really believe I can't? Me? Love itself? Do you honestly believe I won't?

'Remember [in my house there is][4] that room, full of gifts that My children don't want. Please don't add yours to the pile.

'Love Me, for all the reasons love exists. All that is in creation, in nature, in families, in the kind-hearted, in human giving, all of it, is from Me. Just Me. Don't rely on others for what they have received from Me. Receive it for yourself.

'What is it you want from a man?

'Love – I've covered that.

'Affection – I dote on you.

'Passion – I'm crazy about you. Look how much I've poured out on you! Talent, leadership, evangelism, joy, the ability to love others wholeheartedly. Enthusiasm, humour, honesty, purity, strong will, passion itself.

'Protection – underneath you are My everlasting arms.[5] When you walk in My shadow, nothing will harm you.[6] The protection of My love.

'Commitment – I will never leave you or forsake you.[7]

'Value – I died for you. You were on My mind as I hung. You have a passport to heaven, given to you, just because I chose you as you are. You have, are and will be used to bring others to Me. Look at My promises! You will find lost sheep and bring them to Me.

'Love others. Unconditionally. And I'll give you more and more and more...

'Right now I need you to be patient. I need you to struggle so that you will come back to Me. I need a testimony from you. You are not allowed to find someone yourself because that is not faith or trust. So I will not allow you to even look. Trust Me and I will deliver My promise. I will make it clear as day. I will knock your door down against all resistance so you know for sure it is My delivery, not your invention.

'My gift, your pleasure.

'Wait.'

Get real with God

I'd like to encourage you to take some time out to think about what you have read so far and spend a little one-on-one time with Jesus. Grab a Bible, some paper and a pen. Lie down, sit or go for a walk somewhere you won't bump into anyone. Climb a hill early in the morning like Jesus did if that works for you. Go to your church and sit somewhere you won't be disturbed. Whichever way you usually connect best with God, may I encourage you to do so now? Worship. Pray. Listen.

You may or may not be used to listening to God for answers so if you're not, maybe try what I did and imagine that Jesus is standing in front of you, talking – what might He say in this moment? Then write it down. Don't worry if it's right or wrong, you or God – that will become clear later. Just write it down. Ask two questions. Then write the answers. Ask:

Lord, how much do You love me?
Lord, what were You thinking of when you made me?

Alternatively, write a letter to God, telling Him everything you feel about this topic – whether your feelings are good, bad, healthy or unhealthy, remember, it doesn't matter – God can handle that. Tell Him what you really want.

Then write everything you want out of your relationship with God and offer it up to Him. You can speak, shout or sing it aloud to the heavens, or write it, put it in an envelope with His name on, or in a diary, or email it to yourself and store it in a folder labelled 'Jesus'. Whichever way you do it, I encourage you to give it to Him.

Chapter Eight
Boundaries and Waiting

Where has your beloved gone,
Oh fairest among women?
Where has your beloved turned aside,
That we may seek him with you?
(Song of Solomon 6:1)

The last chapter ended with words spoken to me from God, and then an encouragement for you to listen to God yourself. Some of you will find that totally natural and normal and some will find it completely out there. So, very briefly, let me reassure you. Maybe one day I'll write a whole book about it, but God speaking to His children is completely normal and to be expected (John 8:47; Jeremiah 33:3; Psalm 25:14; John 14:26; Acts 2:17–18 for starters).

Being able to discern His thoughts from our own thoughts is where many of us can get in a tangle. How do you know if God has spoken to you, or if it was just your own imagination? There are three tests you can put it through[1] but, in the end, God Himself reveals the ultimate test to every prophetic word in Deuteronomy 18:21–22:

> You may say to yourselves, 'How can we know when a message has not been spoken by the Lord?' If what a prophet proclaims in the name of the Lord does not take place or come true, that is a message the Lord has not spoken. That prophet has spoken presumptuously, so do not be alarmed.

Sometimes we worry too much about figuring out the difference between our thoughts and God's thoughts, but this verse tells us that if it's not God, it won't happen. If it is God, it will. Until then, offer the words back to God and trust His timing. But if you're still worried, read a book or two from my recommended reading list at the end.

Looking back to 'The Promise'

When I first wrote the words of 'The Promise' I considered them to be helpful, but now I consider them to be profound. Why? Mostly because...

EVERYTHING THE LORD SPOKE TO ME ON THAT DAY HAS COME TRUE.

Also, because they passed the three tests of prophecy (see end notes again).

Over the years I have read 'The Promise' aloud to others and had the most amazing feedback – those words have brought hope and clarity and helped others in their journey of looking for love. Ultimately, 'The Promise' was so powerful because it turned my journey of looking for love on its head. God revealed to me through scripture after scripture how He was the one I had been looking for all along. He is the supplier of my needs and the fulfiller of my heart's desires. He showed me that by trusting Him, putting Him first, He would provide for me what I needed, when I needed it, in a way I would know it was from Him.

Some of those words were personal – like the specific gifts He has given me – but others are true for everyone. While our journeys may look different, there are principles that are the same for us all.

What are some of the principles that are common to everyone? Let's start with two: boundaries and waiting. These are not the main focus of this book, but they're important and definitely worthy of their own chapter!

Boundaries

My first reaction after writing the words of 'The Promise' was to put a rule in place. I decided I would not date for six months. I broke it two weeks later. After dumping that two-week boyfriend, I came back to my diary, scribbled out the original six-month deadline and wrote a new one six months from then. OK, God, this time I mean it!

Some boundaries exist because God has put them in place for everyone's benefit and these don't change no matter who we are, where we live, or what generation we are born into. Keeping sex within a marriage is an example of a universal boundary put in place by God for all people, all the time, for our benefit.[2] Not marrying a brother, sister, stepbrother or stepsister, parent or stepparent, grandparent, auntie, uncle or in-law[3] are other universal boundaries put in place by God for all people, all the time, for our benefit.

Other boundaries we put in place ourselves to help us through a specific situation and they're more personal and can change as circumstances change. They don't work for everyone, all the time; they are really just for your own self, some of the time. They're not God's laws and it is not sin to break them, but occasionally they might help you in your area of weakness. Let me explain.

When we are children, we have very strong boundaries put in place by our parents. 'Don't touch that', 'Say please', 'Hold my hand while we cross the road please'. Why? Because our parents love us and they want us to grow up unharmed and with a good character. As we get older the boundaries relax and we get more opportunities to make our own choices, express our preferences and opinions. Eventually most people are mature enough to live life without needing to ask Mum or Dad what they think before making every single decision (*most* people).

While we are young in our faith or immature about certain issues, we too may find strong boundaries helpful.

I NEEDED SOME STRONG BOUNDARIES WHEN IT CAME TO RELATIONSHIPS BECAUSE I SIMPLY DIDN'T KNOW HOW TO DO THEM WELL.

I didn't know how to make a healthy friendship with a male and I didn't know how I should be looking for love. So when the Lord spoke to me so powerfully that day of 'The Promise', He asked me to stop looking for love.

Actually, He didn't ask me to stop looking for love, He asked me to stop trying to find a husband. And that is quite a different thing. He gently tried to turn my head to stop looking at men to fulfil the deep down desire of my heart and to instead look to Him.

Fast dating

Some people think it might be a good idea to stop dating for a while, if you have actually been dating, of course. Some people make it a law that everyone ought to follow ('All Christians should not date ever') but I think that it is more of a personal matter, or sometimes a community matter,[4] that is helpful for some people, for a specific period of time. If you feel weak or immature in this area of your life, you might decide it would be really helpful for you to take a break from dating for a while, in order to allow God to be your strength and help you grow in maturity. This type of thing is not so much a rule or a law but a fast. A fast is usually when you stop eating or drinking something for a specific time in order to strengthen your prayers and prepare your heart for something God wants to teach you. But you can fast more than just food – we've already mentioned the bit in the Bible about married couples fasting sex (1 Corinthians 7:5), but it is only for a limited time because married couples should be having sex.

Perhaps you sense somewhere inside you that God is prompting you to fast dating. If you are not feeling that, don't worry about it – it's a decision between you and God and no one else. But if you do think a few more boundaries in this area of weakness (if it is a weakness of yours, like it was mine) would be helpful right now, here are some tips to make the most of it:

• Don't think of it as a law, a rule, or a commandment that everyone ought to do. And don't do it to look good in God's eyes – or anyone else's for that matter. Think of it like giving up chocolate for Lent. Whenever you feel hungry (or horny!) change your focus, look up and talk to God instead – not about your need, but about something else; pray for a loved one to know Jesus or for peace in Israel – anything to change your focus away from your need and up towards Jesus.
• Make yourself accountable to someone else. Ask a woman who is more spiritually mature than you, someone you trust, to meet with you or write/Skype/FaceTime/email you regularly and pray for you daily.
• Give it a deadline. Six weeks, six months or a year maybe. When there is a light at the end of the tunnel, it's easier to keep going, even when it's hard. At the end of the deadline, you can ask God what to do next. Perhaps by then you'll have grown in this area and can move onto the next stage, or perhaps you'll need to extend your strong boundaries for a bit longer.
• Fully expect it to be tested and if you break it, just come back to God and start again. Remember, it's a voluntary fast, not a law. There is no commandment that says 'Thou shalt not date'! Just try again.

If you are the kind of person who doesn't date but perhaps you struggle in your thoughts – perhaps you spend too much time fantasising about being married, perhaps you look at young men as 'potentials' instead of human beings, or perhaps you have lustful thoughts, or doubt God loves you or will provide for you, or thoughts that you are not worthy of God's love or provision. All these thoughts can be fasted too. Read through those principles again and apply the same guidelines.

A mind fast is harder than a physical fast, but that just means it's more powerful! It is how you overcome the enemy:

> The weapons we fight with are not the weapons of the world. On the contrary, they have divine power to demolish strongholds. We demolish arguments and every pretension that sets itself up against the knowledge of God, and we take captive every thought to make it obedient to Christ. (2 Corinthians 10:4–5, NIV UK 2011)

Waiting

Whether or not you 'fast dating' for a while is your choice. Periods of waiting, however, usually happen to you, whether you like it or not. We are all definitely going to have times of waiting in our lives – waiting for God to provide, waiting for Him to fulfil His promises to us, or being engaged and waiting till your wedding day (and night!). As a culture, we don't like to wait. At theme parks, you can pay ridiculous amounts of money to buy passes or tickets that mean you don't have to queue for as long as everyone else. If you are meeting a friend in town and are running late, you'll get a text within one minute of the deadline, saying: 'Where are you?!?!?' In a book by Dr Seuss called *Oh, The Places You'll Go!*[5] the waiting room is considered a 'useless place' to 'escape from' as quickly as possible or you'll be considered a failure.

In spite of all that, knowing our culture and our weakness for waiting, sometimes the Lord asks us to wait. Sometimes it seems the Lord is quiet for a while. Sometimes, often when we need Him most, it seems He is far away or not listening. Let me show you three examples in the Bible to help us understand what God is actually doing during those times, and what we can do to make the most of it.

1. Job – waiting for understanding

First, Job. The book of Job is really long – forty-two chapters, in fact. God features in the first twelve verses of the first chapter and then He is silent till chapter 38 when He suddenly has a lot to say! Those thirty-seven and a half chapters might have only been a few days or weeks, but as you read them, they seem to go on forever. What is God doing during those thirty-seven chapters? We know what Job is doing: suffering, defending himself, waiting, waiting, waiting. We also know what his friends are doing: blaming, yelling, accusing, coming up with theories and doctrines based on guesses, trying to rationalise what seems so irrational. (They can't accept that a good person would suffer, so if Job was suffering it must be his own fault). Don't we too come up with all kinds of crazy reasons why God hasn't blessed us with a boyfriend yet? It must be because we've done something wrong. It must be because we don't have enough faith. It must be because we want it too much etc., etc.

So what is God doing? I believe God was waiting too – waiting for a testimony so that He could tell the whole world the same thing at the end of the story that He said at the beginning: 'Look at My servant, Job! See how he trusts in Me! Even when everything else is telling him not to; his circumstances, his best friends and even his wife tells him to curse Me and die [Job 2:9] but Job says he will trust Me anyway. That's my boy!'

However, Job's life isn't exactly the same as yours – singleness is not an affliction like skin boils or losing your children. In fact, in all Job's sufferings the one thing he kept was his wife! (So maybe marriage is a greater 'affliction' than singleness? I'm joking! Maybe... No, really, I'm joking. Or am I? I can't decide). Let's look at someone else's story.

2. Noah – waiting for the next stage of the journey

After God told Noah to go into the ark with his family and all the animals in Genesis 7:1, the rain started. It rained for forty days and nights and then it stopped, but that was not the end of the story. In Genesis 7:24 we read that the water 'prevailed on the earth' for 150 days before God then remembered Noah (8:1). Then it was still another 150 days before the ark rested on Mount Ararat (8:3–4), another two and a half months before they could see the tops of other mountains (8:5) and then Noah waited another forty days before he sent out the raven, then the dove. Then another seven days before he sent the dove again, then another seven before he sent it again and it never came back. Then on the first day of the following year, after the waters had finally dried up in the earth, Noah waited another month and twenty-seven days before finally, at long last, after 370 days[6] of silence, God finally spoke. He told Noah he could get off the ark (8:14–17).

Three hundred and seventy days is a long time of waiting while you are in the most critical period of your life. During that time, God said absolutely nothing to Noah. God had not forgotten Noah – when God 'remembered' Noah it meant God was ready to do something, not that He'd forgotten about him.

What was God doing? He was preparing the ground for Noah and his family to survive. What was Noah doing? Noah was getting on with the job he'd been given till God told him to stop.

WAITING IS HARD, BUT IT IS NEVER POINTLESS.

After a seed has been planted, you don't see anything for a while but it's all happening underneath the surface – new life is getting ready to spring up! There's more growth in our character during times of seeming 'inaction' on God's part than at any other time in our lives. It's the butterfly in the chrysalis all over again – you don't see the butterfly till it's ready to fly, but it's growing stronger in that secret, hidden place every day.

So what is God doing while you wait? He might be preparing the ground for your future, like with Noah. He might be waiting too, like with Job, waiting for a testimony from you so you can say: 'My God is faithful!'

You see, even when God is silent, nothing of real importance has changed. He still loves you. Jesus still died for you. Your value remains the same as it was on the day He sacrificed Himself on the cross for you. The truth hasn't changed, God's character hasn't changed and His will for your life hasn't changed.

What do we do during the waiting? We can do what Job did and hold strong. We can decide not to cave in to the pressures to sin from our friends and culture – a culture that doesn't understand God. We can do what Noah did and just carry on doing the stuff that the Lord has given us to do (Ephesians 2:10).

Waiting doesn't mean being idle and it certainly doesn't mean putting your life on hold till you're married – it means being ready. Like a waitress at a restaurant, she is not idle; she is very busy getting on with her job and she is constantly ready for the voice that might call her for her next task – whatever that might be.

Waiting also means keeping yourself available for God. So when He calls, you can answer straight away without having any messes to sort out first. It might just be that if you fill your single years with a string of 'The Wrong Ones' you may not be ready or available at the right time, or have to wait a little longer.

3. Abraham – waiting for the promise to be fulfilled

There is a third family in the Bible who God asked to trust Him and wait. It was the family of Abraham and Sarah. God promised Abraham a son of his own (Genesis 15:4) and Abraham believed Him (15:6). Later, after a lot of waiting, Sarah miraculously conceived Isaac, the child of the promise. But did Abraham and Sarah wait well? They did for a while, but then they didn't. They conceived an Ishmael. They decided (like Dr Seuss!) it was a fool's game to wait and that if you want something you should make it happen yourself. After all, hasn't God given us brains and muscles and sex organs to do these things? But Ishmael was a human effort to fulfil a God-promise, and while God still loved Ishmael, took care of him and blessed him with his own nation, Ishmael was not the son of the promise. Ever since then, even till today, the descendants of Ishmael have rarely been at peace with the descendants of Isaac.

How can this story help us with our twenty-first century love lives? Let's look at this in the next chapter.

Get real with God

If you feel prompted to put any temporary relationship boundaries in place, what might they be?

Do you have a mature, female, Christian mentor that you can trust? Who might you ask?

Have you ever had to wait for something? How did you cope?

Was there anything in this chapter that could help you wait better?

Chapter Nine
The Almost Right One

What is your beloved
More than another beloved,
O fairest among women?
What is your beloved
More than another beloved,
That you so charge us [to find him]?
(Song of Solomon 5:9)

There is more than one kind of test in this area of relationships. Remember the three guys from chapter one? First was the right kind of guy, then was the wrong kind of guy and then there were the nice guys, the 'almost right' guys – the Ishmaels.

Perhaps you passed the test of 'The Wrong One' because he was so obviously wrong. Or perhaps you fell for 'The Wrong One' once and are determined not to fall for another one, so you are very good at avoiding the wrong kind of men. But there are many, many, many young men out there who 'might' be right for you, and how do you know which one God has picked for you? Do you shut yourself away and wait for a divine knock on the door from 'The One'?

For starters, I don't believe in the concept of 'The One' unless you are talking about Jesus Christ. God says 'I know the plans I have for you', not 'The Plan' (Jeremiah 29:11, NLT). But I do believe in arranged marriages – arranged by our Father God, that is. I do believe that if we allow God to be Lord of our love lives, He will pick us a better choice than we would pick for ourselves. After all, He knows us better than we know ourselves and He knows everyone else in the world too (Psalm 139). And His intentions are always for good (Romans 8:28; Jeremiah 29:11) and His end goal is always love.

GOD IS THE MOST HIGHLY QUALIFIED MATCHMAKER IN EXISTENCE...

...don't you think?

At some point in your life, you may have given your heart to Jesus. But did you take that literally? Let me explain what I mean by that with the remaining part of my story.

Giving my heart to Jesus

So I was waiting. I'd made a commitment to God not to date for six months (which for me was a huge deal) and I was really enjoying life. All my efforts were focused on God and the stuff He had given me to do at that time, and we were getting along great. I went on a snowboarding holiday to Sweden with a bunch of friends from university and I didn't even flirt with the new boys I met, even though they were good-looking, single, and they were Bible college students. You couldn't get more eligible than that! But I didn't flirt even one bit. (I was so pleased with myself I wrote it in my diary!)

But I did start to get along very well with one of them. *Very* well. We kept in touch after the holiday because he only lived in the next town. We had a lot in common; in fact, I thought we were very similar in lots of ways. I asked advice from some good friends about what to do with these feelings and they recommended I put up barriers. They said to me, if this young man was God's choice for me, no man-made barrier would prevent it from being a successful relationship, but if a simple barrier was too much for the relationship to overcome, then it was clearly not from God. This, by the way, is excellent advice. A bit like when Isaac's servant was looking for Rebekah. Remember in Genesis 24 Abraham's servant was sent to find a wife for Isaac and he asked God to show him the right woman? He asked God for a sign of incredible generosity that went above and beyond the norm, a sign that would convince him that this girl was God's choice.

So what could I use for a barrier? Well, I was still in my six-month 'fast' so I decided that if he asked me out on the very day that my waiting commitment was over, I would take that as a sign and say yes. I thought that was quite a good barrier at the time. (Can you spot the flaw in that plan? No? You will...)

So we didn't go out on any dates or talk about feelings (much), but we did spend lots of time together, mostly in groups with other friends. So far, so good. As the day of my 'fast' came to end, I managed to work it out so that we would be alone together in an ultra-romantic setting and *voila*! It worked! He told me he liked me and we became boyfriend and girlfriend. Surely, I thought, this must be God! Right? Well, maybe not.

Here was the flaw in the plan. While I had 'technically' kept my boundary of six months of no dating in place, I was secretly exerting all my efforts so that by the time the deadline came, he would be ready to go out with me. He didn't really want to – he liked me but he also really liked being single, and I actually manipulated the circumstances a bit (if you ever read this, I'm sorry). I suppose I really liked this boy and wasn't completely convinced God would do His bit in getting us together, so I gave God a helping hand. Just like Sarah did when she gave up waiting for God to fulfil His promise of a child and told Abraham to make a child with her maidservant, Hagar, instead. The result was not the child of the promise and a lot of people got very hurt in this man-made attempt to 'help' God fulfil His promise (read the full story in in Genesis 16 and 21).

Just like Dr Seuss and pretty much all Western culture tells us, I made my own future and attributed it to divine power. I said

I HAD GIVEN MY HEART TO JESUS BUT WHEN IT CAME TO THE CRUNCH, I TOOK MY LOVE LIFE BACK INTO MY OWN HANDS.

Three months into this relationship, while I'm still convinced this is the man God has chosen for me, God asks me, 'Would you give this young man up for Me?' I was sitting on my bed and I had come to recognise this stirring in my soul as the Lord speaking to my heart. I answered, in my heart.

'But Lord, he's not like that other guy who was The Wrong One. This one is a Christian. We even pray together!'

'I know. Would you give him up for Me?'

'But I like him. He's so good for me! Didn't You give him to me, Lord?'

'Will you give him up for Me anyway?'

'Hang on, is this one of those times like when You asked Abraham to sacrifice his son Isaac and then You said he didn't have to actually do it, once You saw he had a willing heart? Can I just say yes and then You'll say I don't have to after all? You know, the whole "letting something go so it will come back to you" kind of thing?'

'Maybe. Maybe not. Will you give him up for Me?'

I wrestled with this in my heart for a while.

The pearl necklace

Do you know the story of the girl and the pearl necklace? There was once a little girl who saved up her pocket money to buy a necklace from the toy shop that looked like it was made of real pearls. She treasured the necklace. But one night her daddy asks her: 'Do you love me?' She replies, 'Yes, Daddy.' So he asks her, 'Will you give me your pearl necklace?' She replies, 'You know I love you, but I can't give you my pearl necklace.'

He goes away and comes back the next night to ask again. 'Will you give me the pearl necklace?' She replies, 'Daddy you know I love you, but I don't understand why you want my pearl necklace. I can't give it to you.'

On the third night the daddy asks her again, 'Do you love me?

Will you give me the pearl necklace?' She replies, 'Daddy, I love my pearl necklace, but I also love you more. I don't understand why you are asking for it, but if you want it so much, I'll give it to you.' It hurts to give up something so precious but he hugs her, thanks her and wipes away her tears. Then he gives her a box. She opens the box and is overjoyed to find a *real* pearl necklace inside as his gift to her – a gift worth 1,000 times more from a daddy who thought her true worth was priceless.

Trusting God with your love life

I knew that if God was asking me to give something to Him, there was a good reason for it. That reason was more than I could understand in the moment of giving. In the end, I had to decide, who do I trust more with my heart? Me? My boyfriend? Or my Lord, my God, my Creator, the one who knows me and loves me above anyone else? In the end, there was only one answer I could give.

'OK, Lord. I'll give my boyfriend up to You. If I get to keep him or if I lose him, it's up to You now. My heart belongs to You.'

The very next time I saw my boyfriend he broke up with me. Actually, I had to do the breaking up because he hated hurting people and couldn't find the words to do it! After twenty minutes of sitting together in silence, I cut him some slack and broke up with myself on his behalf. He was very grateful. Bless him.

When Jesus holds your heart

When I broke up with 'The Wrong One' it was the most painful thing I had ever experienced but I was also living in rebellion to God at the time. This time, I was acting out of the opposite of rebellion – submission. And it was totally different.

WHEN JESUS HOLDS YOUR HEART, HE DOESN'T BREAK IT.

Instead of my heart falling and shattering, God held it in His hands so gently and so lovingly. We were actually at this Christian music festival in the north of England and the night before we broke up, I dreamt about co-joined twins being separated, my parents splitting up and finally I dreamed the break-up scene that I then lived through the next day. When I woke up I knew exactly what was coming and I even knew what words to say. God had prepared me, and being prepared somehow cushioned the blow.

You see, I had offered my heart up to this boy and the boy said no. But God was holding it. God held my heart so that instead of it falling, it was slowly lowered back to me. I did cry but I wasn't angry or bitter. I was sad but I was not broken. My heart was not my heart anymore. It belonged to Jesus and He held it.

The real pearl necklace

This was the real turning point in my love life. Before this, I was trying really, really hard to suppress this desire for flirting, to put my love life on the back seat, to ignore my needs and desires and to try to live right. From this point on, I didn't need to try anymore. God had done something. He had changed something inside of me forever – something very deep and fundamental, something that had ruled my behaviour for a long time.

But now it was gone. I didn't need to flirt, I didn't need to hunt for a husband, I didn't need to cry in the mirror over my unmet needs or unfulfilled desires. Jesus had my heart. My love life or lack of it was in His hands and I was free! I was accepted, forgiven, at peace with my God and free. Free to trust God, free to follow where He led me, free to enjoy God and love Him forever. It was incredible.

From that point on, God was my everything. Nothing was hidden or kept from Him anymore. He taught me how to accept a date with a young man, but not give that man my heart. I learned to take God dating with me! I would pray on the way, I would listen to God as the young man talked and I would ask God afterwards – shall I go out with him again or not? God was more than my Saviour now, He was my best friend, and every decision was made after talking with Him about it first.

Bizarrely, I began to find myself on the other side of the looking for love 'hunt'. For example, a new guy started working at the Youth With A Mission (YWAM) national office where I was on placement and he tried to flirt with me. It was weird. I didn't quite know what to do with myself. All I could think was: 'Why are you flirting with me? There's no need for that. That's just silly, stop it.'

Let me finish with one last, funny story (at least to me – not so funny to the poor bloke I was with).

The day 'The Almost Right One' broke up with me, I did what any healthy, mentally balanced young woman would do and bought a bag with the words 'I'm single' written in bright pink lettering on the side for all the world to see. It did wonders for my self-esteem, but then I did something silly. I took it with me to a Christian youth gathering. I may as well have been dangling a raw piece of meat into a piranha tank.

I forget why, but for some reason, I'd been asked to help pass around the bucket for the collection during the preach. I was patiently waiting at the side of the auditorium when the preacher told everyone to turn to their neighbour and say 'You're gorgeous'. At that exact moment, a young man nearby (a young, single Christian man) who had just been lamenting that he couldn't find any young, single Christian women turned to me, saw my bag, heard the preacher make the announcement and something in his brain said, 'There are too many coincidences – this must be God and I have just met my wife.' For the rest of the gathering he stuck to me like glue.

Now, I can't be too rough on the guy because only a few months before I might have done exactly the same thing. But I wasn't that person anymore – I had not gone through the pain of giving up my love life to God in order to be taken in by a few funny circumstances and a boy I'd never met.

We chatted after the concert and he asked me if I'd like to go for a milkshake. I didn't sense a huge warning sign from God not to go so I thought, OK I can go for just a drink. Over our milkshakes he said to me: 'So you must have lots of questions for me.' At first I was confused – why would I have questions for him? – but slowly I realised that he thought he had just met his future wife. He thought I thought this too. So naturally, he thought his future wife might like to get to know him better and would have lots of questions for him.

But no, I was just having a milkshake and a chat. We hung out for a while and exchanged numbers and said goodbye. I prayed and asked God if this was something I should pursue. I wasn't hearing or feeling or thinking anything much, but I agreed to go on one more date just to make sure. The very second I saw him again I knew instantly, without a shadow of a doubt, that I was not attracted to this man. As lovely as he was, I was not interested. So I told him, 'Thank you for the compliment, but I don't think this is going to go anywhere.'

You need to understand something: the old me would never have been able to do that. A few months before, whether or not he was right for me wouldn't have mattered. As long as he was paying me attention and feeding my thirsty soul with the acceptance and love I craved, I would have sucked that boy dry and then awkwardly tried to break up with him – continuing the never-ending cycle of unfulfilment.

But things were different now. I had given up my love life and it had been a hard, painful process. I was not going to go back to that place of manipulating circumstances or remoulding whatever guy walked past me into the perfect man of my dreams. No way.

GOD WAS IN THE DRIVING SEAT OF MY LOVE LIFE NOW.

ᔓᔕ

When Jesus holds your heart, you can get to know a boy without giving him the responsibility or the pressure of holding your heart from the first date. You can take it one date at a time and ask Jesus every step of the way to guide you and make your path clear, and I promise you, He will.

And remember, Jesus is not just the provider of your husband, but He is your provider of all things – whether or not you ever get a husband. He may or He may not return your sacrifice with a husband but He will always, always meet your needs. He is your provider,[1] the fulfiller of your hopes and dreams, the one who meets your deepest needs for love, acceptance, intimacy, security, commitment, adoration, passion, encouragement, appreciation, comfort, joy, peace and love (I put love in there twice, see that?).

Get real with God

Who holds your heart? Does Jesus hold it, or do you keep control of your own love life?

What kind of obstacles might stop you from putting your love life into God's hands? Fear? Doubt? Something else?

What can empower you to overcome these obstacles? (1 John 4:18; 2 Timothy 1:7)

Have you ever tried to give God a helping hand to fulfil His promises over your life?

If you feel able to give your heart to Jesus and make Him Lord of your love life, all it takes is a simple prayer:

Father God,
I trust You. Jesus, as You offered up Your life for me, so I offer my heart and my love life to You. Be my Lord, the fulfiller of my needs. Help me to wait for Your gifts, Your promises and Your guidance. Lead me where You want me to go.
Amen.

Part Three:

Looking At Others: The Faithfulness of God in Real Life

Chapter Ten
God Keeps His Promises

He who has promised is faithful.
(Hebrews 10:23)

I've given up many things to God in my life. I've given Him control over my finances – giving up my faith in money and putting my trust in God to provide, and He has always provided enough with more to spare so I can continue to be generous. When I emigrated to New Zealand to work with YWAM Marine Reach I gave up my home, my country and my family. Again, God provided me with a home, a beautiful country and a loving community. Years later, when God called me back to the UK and to my family, because of births and marriages, it had doubled in size! I've discovered that Jesus was speaking the absolute truth when He said this:

> Assuredly, I say to you, there is no one who has left house or brothers or sisters or father or mother or wife or children or lands, for My sake and the gospel's, who shall not receive a hundredfold now in this time – houses and brothers and sisters and mothers and children and lands, with persecutions – and in the age to come, eternal life.
> (Mark 10:29–30)

In the course of writing this book, I've heard many people's love stories and they all have this in common – there came a time when they had to submit their relationship to God. When they did, sometimes God gave the relationship back to them, even when it seemed past all hope of success. Sometimes, as in my case, He didn't give me the same gift back again, but replaced it with a better one. Some people, however, are called to a single life, like the girls in the next chapter – sometimes for a period of time, sometimes for life. Whichever way God responds to your offering, one thing will always remain true: His character never changes. God is always faithful, always generous, always good, always just and always love.

God is faithful

God does not, never has, and never will need a helping hand to fulfil His promises.

WHAT GOD PROMISES, HE ALWAYS DELIVERS.

God's promises include His strength in our weaknesses (2 Corinthians 12:9). My biggest weakness became the way in which God saved me and transformed my life more dramatically than in any other area of my life. He didn't transform me from a single girl to a married woman – that's just demographics! God transformed me from an unhappy, unfulfilled, desperate girl to a submitted woman who trusted her heavenly Father with her love life and rested in that knowledge.

God also promised me a gift, and this is how He delivered it.

One day, I was invited to join the YWAM King's Kids team at Spring Harvest in Skegness to help look after the eight to eleven-year-olds. My friend Charlie convinced me to go. He said that if I came it would change my life. And it did.

One the first day, all the helpers met together and there were about fifty of us. One girl next to me leaned over and said, 'My friend thinks he recognises you from somewhere – do you know him?' I looked over and saw a man who did look strangely familiar, but I couldn't place him. His name was Johnny G and the girl was a member of a new Christian band called TBC, launching at Spring Harvest that week. Johnny G was their manager.

Our team of fifty helpers got to know each other over the next ten days and hung out a lot in our spare time. The girls from TBC were a lot of fun and joined in and Johnny G was always around. At one point we exchanged numbers because I had a contact at a Christian Radio station I was willing to share with him, to help promote the band. I didn't really think much of it at the time. The next day, I found myself walking with Johnny G and my room-mate, Joanna, on the Skegness beach. I wondered if there was anything in it but when I mentioned it to another friend, Claire, she told me that she had walked on the beach with him too, the day before. So I brushed off the idea of Johnny G liking me, thinking he was just a friendly guy who liked walks on the beach. What I didn't realise was that he did like me, had asked me for my number and was trying very hard to get my attention (including getting to know my friends so he could ask them about me, hence the walks on the beach). I don't know if he ever did call my radio contact.

Joanna and I stuck together most of that conference and bumped into Johnny G a lot. I think it was day six or seven that she pointed out that we had had two very long, unplanned conversations with him in one day. I retorted, 'Well, it's you or me he fancies, then!' I was just being facetious but I think Joanna knew. I think she could see a mile away that this guy was not just 'bumping into us' three times a day, but that he was deliberately trying to spend time with me. In fact, almost every single day he asked me if I'd like to go for a drink with him and I would say, 'Sure, I'll see you in the team lounge after the kids' session.' I don't think a weak orange squash with the other fifty helpers in a brightly lit room was what he meant – he meant at one of the onsite bars or cafés – but I just assumed he was being friendly, nothing more.

Why didn't I notice it? Why didn't I notice that the future love of my life, father of my children, husband and best friend was trying to sweep me off my feet while I kept dodging the broom? This is the girl who noticed every single Christian man within a three-mile radius and assumed a nice gesture or prolonged look meant true love. I can only put it down to the fact that God had transformed my life, renewed my mind and kept my heart in His hands.

It wasn't till the second-to-last day when Johnny asked me for a walk on the beach (to which I brought three friends along) that he finally plucked up the courage to say something to me. Just as he had separated me from the others and was about to speak – his phone rang! While he answered it, I ran off to join the others, giving him some privacy. That night he texted me: 'Hey you, I tried to talk to you on the beach today but you ran off. You scared or something? Can we go for a drink tonight?' The penny dropped. A drink? He means, like a date? Not in the team lounge, but in the bar area in the main building... maybe with alcohol? Suddenly I was very nervous and unsure. It was 9pm and I was thinking of going to bed, but it was our last night before the conference ended so instead, for the first time all week, I put make-up on and headed for the bar.

So we had a drink. Joanna came and found me alone at the table with two glasses of wine in front of me (Johnny had momentarily disappeared to pick up some microphones after TBC had done their final concert). She got so excited that I was on a date with Johnny G that she knelt down and prayed for me right then and there. I was shocked that she was so excited. 'He's a great guy, you know,' she said, meaningfully.

After our date we joined some of the others for a midnight stroll on the beach again – one last time together before the end of a life-changing ten days teaching kids all about God. Johnny tried to put his arm around me but I was very unsure about him at this point, so shrugged it off. Back in our room, Joanna and Claire wanted all the girly details about what was going on with me and Johnny G and we did something I never expected – we prayed together!

My history with boys had been so filled with bad choices that praying usually consisted of: 'I'm sorry, God. I did it again.' This kind of praying was new and exciting – prayer about this wonderful new relationship and asking God to guide me about what to do next.

As soon as I closed my eyes, a moving image of a wedding filled my mind and I heard the words as clear as day (without being actually audible): 'My gift.' Still, I was reluctant to accept this gift and I silently said to the Lord, 'Are you talking about Johnny G, or are you speaking metaphorically about someone else when I'm older? You can't mean right here, right now?'

But He did. God had knocked down my door against all resistance. This man had asked me out every day for nine days, followed me around, bought me gifts, bought me a drink or two, bought glue to fix a broken trinket of mine, took me (and all my friends!) for walks on the beach and I hadn't seen what was so obvious to everyone else. Even when God was calling out to me – 'This is My gift to you!' – I couldn't quite take it in.

Johnny was my gift from the Father. It took me just two weeks to fall in love and six weeks later we were engaged. That was May 2004. Sixteen months later we were married. Johnny was not my prize for waiting faithfully (as you saw, I was rubbish at waiting). He was not my reward for a spiritually mature life. Meeting and marrying him did not mean I had attained some spiritual status. He was not my goal, but he was my gift. Johnny was a gift from the Giver, my provider, the Trinity called Love.

God had promised He would knock down every door and He did. Johnny and I had a long-distance relationship from the day we met till the day we married, but it was never a burden or barrier. In fact, it helped us grow stronger by teaching us to communicate better.

God also promised me a testimony. So on my wedding day, I broke protocol and gave a speech, glorifying the God who keeps His promises. I read aloud 'The Promise' and received a standing ovation. Not because I had done anything special, but because God had shown Himself faithful to His promises and I wanted my wedding day to glorify God and praise His faithfulness. Over the years, as I've shared parts of this story with others, they have been blessed and thanked me for helping them and pointing them towards Jesus. Then at thirty-one years old, God said, 'It's time to write it down.' And you're reading it now. God's promises keep going and going.

Just like with Noah, Job and Abraham – God is still faithful

Remember how Johnny's first communication with me was that I looked familiar? That's because the previous summer, in another town called Nuneaton, we had both eaten in the same lounge with only a dozen or so other people, most of whom I'd never met since. So at Spring Harvest, he really did recognise and remember me, even though to this day I still don't remember him. Perhaps it was because at that time, I had only just broken up with 'The Almost Right One' and was a bit distracted with my own grief. In fact, Johnny had stood behind me in a marquee while I cried on my friend's shoulder at the sadness of my break-up. Johnny remembers seeing me crying and he remembers a joke I made over lunch, but he never spoke to me.

A few months after that, and still a few months before we properly met at Spring Harvest, we were once again at the same event in yet another city, this time Liverpool. I was there taking photos for my work and – can you believe it? – he is there in my photos! Before we properly met, I took photos of him singing on stage as part of the worship team. Why didn't we meet then, or the time before? I have no idea. Perhaps it just wasn't the right time.

But that part of our story really tells me something – God was on the case! He was already working on my behalf, putting in place the fulfilment of His promises, long before I was ever aware of it. Like when Noah was on the boat, there was work going on under the surface that he couldn't see. Similar to Job (though on a much smaller scale), God had brought me through times of testing so that I could have a testimony of His faithfulness to me. Johnny was a part of my life long before I met him. God was preparing us both for each other and when the time was right, we met.

Finally, like Abraham waiting for Isaac, God's timing was better than mine and His fulfilment of His own promise was better than my own attempts. I used to look at Johnny in those early days and thank God He had asked me to give up the 'Almost Right One' because there was simply no comparison between the two men. Johnny was more than I could have asked for or even imagined. (That sounds like a Bible verse... I think you'll find it is! Ephesians 3:20).

Who has my heart now?

So does Jesus still have my heart, or does Johnny have it now? Is the journey of looking for love over once you're engaged? What about when you're married? Do we still need Jesus in charge of our love lives, or was He just a caretaker till the husband came along to take over? No, I don't believe Jesus is the caretaker and let me tell you why.

About two weeks before my wedding day I woke from a bad dream. I was dreaming about the craziness of the situation I was in. I was about to leave my family who had been there since forever and join myself with a relative stranger. I was about to commit the rest of my life – be it one year or eighty-nine years – to someone I had only known for eighteen months. Suddenly, it seemed absurd. So I prayed. And God flooded my heart with peace and reminded me that He had chosen Johnny for me and He had chosen me for Johnny. My faith was not in Johnny – it was in my Father, my husband-maker, the Lord of my life and my love life. I discovered that even though I was getting married, my faith would never be transferred from God to my husband – in fact, I was about to enter a stage of life when I was going to need God in new ways I had never imagined before (remember chapter five?).

I had already given my heart to the one who knew me most and loved me more. He had swept the earth with His eyes and found me someone who would be good for me, and when I agreed to marry that someone,

I WAS TAKING A STEP OF FAITH – NOT FAITH IN MY HUSBAND, BUT FAITH IN GOD AND HIS PLAN FOR ME.

My security was not in my husband. It was in God. My trust was not that my husband would remain faithful to me, but that God would remain faithful to me, no matter what.

This is why trusting God with the single-most important relationship of your life is so important. Because if you decide to go a different way, to stop following Jesus on the path He's called you to walk, to turn off at the junction of 'The Wrong One' or be diverted by an 'Almost Right One', then what happens when that person (the one you chose over Jesus) lets you down? Even marrying a good choice, a compatible choice, a God-given gift won't protect you from the times a husband will let you down. For example, my darling husband, Johnny, is a gift and a dream come true, but I remember one moment in particular when he let me down. All my love for him seemed to fall out of my heart in an instant and all I had left was Jesus and His faithfulness. I clung to my pillow as I clung to my Lord and prayed so hard in that black moment. Thankfully, it turned out not to be that big of a deal and we got through it stronger than ever, but I remember that moment so vividly – it shocked me that I could feel that way about my husband, and all I could think was, 'Thank You, God, that my trust is in You, that my foundation is in You, that You never change or stop loving me and that You are forever faithful.'

May I encourage you now, if I haven't done so enough already, to give your heart to Jesus and don't take it back for a lesser man.

Never to give up the Faithful One for an unfaithful one, the Perfect Man for an imperfect man, the Source of All Love for a fleeting taste of emotion.

How do you know when you've met the right one?

So how do you know the young man in front of you is God's choice and not just your overactive imagination, or hormones, or desperation speaking? How can you tell between a Wrong One, a Good One or an Almost Right One?

First of all, I believe God speaks to each of us in our own language, in ways we can understand. Jesus said, 'My sheep hear My voice' (see John 10:2-16 & 27). Good Bible teaching about discerning God's voice will certainly help, but even without that, God knows how to get through to you.

I tried to come up with a list of principles for 'How do you know', but it was impossible. The details of our journeys are all so different and no two couples have exactly the same story. Ultimately, all I can tell you is how I knew Johnny was right for me. I hope that my list of reasons reassures you that God will provide you with plenty of confirmation in ways you will recognise and understand, just like He did for me.

Johnny was a good head decision first. The night I found out Johnny liked me, my close friend Joanna encouraged me, saying he was a really good guy and worth considering. So in my head, I made a decision to give him a chance and see what my heart had to say. Over the next week, my heart began to open up to him and fall in love with him. Then Johnny did something for me that was so generous and so self-sacrificing[1] that my head and heart came together and said, 'If this guy is willing to do this for me, he is a good choice and I want to give him my heart too.' There was no battle between head and heart, it was a decision of my whole being.

Prayer. God spoke to me through prayer several times and each time came the words 'My gift'. These words carried a lot of personal meaning, as you know. Then, just before we got engaged, we prayed and asked our heavenly Father's permission to marry and God gave us both a vision in our minds that was identical to the other. This was one more confirmation, in a way I personally valued.

A sense of peace. Previously, I had often felt confused in relationships that had basically begun in lust. But the night Johnny and I started our relationship, we were sitting together in my lounge and a thick sense of holiness saturated the room. He didn't try anything on, we just talked and he stroked my hair and I felt so safe, so peaceful, like God was in the room, filling it with His purity, His peace, His presence, His holiness.

I know many couples who have their own list of confirmations that are completely different to mine. Ultimately, if my list has not been helpful and you are still unsure, ask God to make it clear in a way you will understand. Trust Him – He can do it because He knows you. He knows how you think, feel, and how you make decisions. He can make your path straight (Proverbs 3:5-6), He is a light to your path and a lamp to your feet (Psalm 119:105).

Have you ever experienced God's guidance in your life? How did you know God was guiding you?

Has God ever asked you to give something up for Him? Did He give it back to you? Or did He replace it with something better? Or are you still waiting?

Think about times in your life when God has shown you His faithfulness, His generosity or His love. How many can you think of?

In the Bible, when has God show Himself to be faithful or generous?

Chapter Eleven
The Value of a Single Life

So the person who marries his fiancée does well, and the person who doesn't marry does even better.
(1 Corinthians 7:38, NLT)

Not everyone experiences marriage, but everyone experiences being single.

ഌ

My nanna had a thirty-five-year marriage that only ended when my grandad died. That sounds like a long and successful marriage, doesn't it? But Nanna lived to be ninety-six – that means for sixty-one years of her life she was single. This really challenges me about the value of singleness – that even someone who has a long and (I assume) happy marriage could still spend two-thirds of their lives being unmarried.

As a woman who married at twenty-three, and is currently only thirty-four, I do not feel I can speak with authority about the value of remaining single for a long period of time, so I've asked a couple of friends to help me out.

Back in 2007 I shared an office with two beautiful young women while we were all in our mid-late twenties, serving with Marine Reach in Tauranga, New Zealand. I'd like to hand this chapter over to them.

Esther's story

Esther is a beautiful Dutch nurse who has devoted her entire life to serving God through medical missions in three continents. She loves her family and friends, is always quick to pray and is the best encourager I know. You've already met her in this book. She married at thirty-three after thirteen years of being single.

Can you describe to me the struggles you have had with being single?

I always thought I would marry young. But after a break-up with a long-term boyfriend when I was eighteen (and apart from a brief six-week relationship in my twenties) I remained single till I was thirty-one when I began a relationship with Maarten.

The desire for a husband went up and down over the years. Sometimes it's been a very strong desire and other times I was completely at peace being single.

In my early twenties, my longing for a companion was more painful at times. I've felt a desire to be a missionary from a very young age, but I've always been afraid that I would be this stereotypical single missionary in Africa for the rest of my life. In the years after my break-up, God healed my heart and regularly spoke to me about putting my right to get married on the altar; to surrender to God's ways and also to accept being single for the rest of my life. It took me years to get there, not with my head but with my heart, but I think I finally could do that – to really put it on the altar and to say, 'OK, God, not my will but Your will be done.' I decided to trust God that He has my future in His hands and that He has the best for me. Then the fear left and the peace came. It was really freeing.

Did the desire to get married ever disappear?

No, the desire to get married was still there and the older I got, the more difficult it got to be OK with that. Sometimes going to a wedding, or after watching a movie, I was surprised to find that I felt the pain, the hurt of just being single. I always prayed, 'God you have to take this away! I can't function like this!' Then most of the time, actually in a few days, the peace came again. Through the years these painful times became shorter and shorter and most of the time within a day of feeling that pain I felt God – I felt His peace and His comfort covering my heart again, and I could just enjoy and grasp and fully engage the single time that I had.

Did you believe you would get married some day?
I always believed that God had a husband for me. I believed that but, of course, at times, you know after years and years I would sometimes doubt.

Why did you still believe you would get married?
That's something that I guess deep in my spirit or in my heart God just put there.

Then there wasn't a special word of prophecy or anything like that...
Oh, yes. Yes, there was actually. Funny you should say that! I have had words several times over the years about a husband, but I felt like they were confirmation of what was already in my heart. It is very encouraging to get that. I took them seriously and I wrote them down, but at the same time I held them lightly. I prayed over each one and I gave it back to God and I prayed, 'If this is really a word of prophecy and from You then yes, You will make it happen.' I had to be careful not to try to make them happen myself but just see what God would do and try to live life as normal. Then when I got married I looked back and saw, wow! It was true!

I don't let my life be led by certain words; I see them more as a confirmation about what God is already doing, especially with huge life decisions like that. It will always be a confirmation about what God already spoke to you *clearly* or put in your own heart *clearly*.

But then even in that moment of doubt I would once again be like, 'OK, if I do stay single then I stay single.' It's a bit like going back and forwards; having that desire, but at the same time being content and living in the fullness of life then and there.

And that's a little bit like what I see with others around me who are single. Most of the time they are content, but then you do have those moments when you're down and the desire pops up and you're like, 'Oh no, not again!'

So what do you do when that happens? Pray?
Yes, pray.

Call somebody?
No, just pray. I would be like, 'God! It's back again! You have to help me out again!' And He always did – it never took longer than a week for the peace to come back again.

Did you ever become bitter or angry towards God?
I've fought against becoming bitter and negative and hopeless and I think that's a choice you make – a choice to trust God. But to do that you need that intimacy with God and need to be able to receive His love as well. When you know Him better it's easier to trust Him.

I've seen other people around me being quite bitter and really hurting because they are still single, and I just think it's really the grace of God and not because I did something particularly or I did something well. I really felt that He protected me from bitterness and I could fully be happy for other people when they got married.

Sometimes I did have to work through my own hurt for a day, but then really He always brought me back after a day or a few days to that place of peace and contentment.

What did other people make of you being single for so long?
Sometimes, as I got older, people thought that maybe I was a lesbian. Once or twice someone would ask me if I felt attracted to men. I'm like, 'Yes, I do have that desire for men – I'm just single!' Christians would say, 'You're too picky or too much of a

perfectionist, otherwise you would have got married already.' There might have been some truth in that, but I don't think it has held me back from coming into a relationship. I don't so easily fall in love... some people are in love with this person and then in love with that person, but I was never really like that which I think did protected my heart.

Actually, after the break-up when I was eighteen I had to be set free from not protecting my heart too much and allowing myself to try to date again.

What do you mean?

Well, when I had that break-up, we were planning to get engaged and I really thought I would marry him. I thought he was the man that I received from God, so breaking up was a huge thing for me. My heart was completely broken – I mean, like, completely heartbroken, and it took years for God to fully heal my heart. I was very protective of my heart. But then I began to let that need for self-protection build up walls. I talked with my pastor and he said, 'You have to be careful that this self-protection doesn't become something new that you need to be set free from.'

What happened after that?

There was a guy I really liked for two years and he really liked me so we actually started dating each other, and then after six weeks he broke up with me – but that was fine!

That was actually a kind of freeing experience I needed. I was sad and I cried but I hadn't given my whole heart yet, so it was not like a heart broken. It was actually a good experience in a way for me to not be too self-protective of my own heart. Yeah, it is a risk when you step into a relationship, and you can get hurt. But dating or not dating – that is a whole other discussion!

What are some of the different ideas you have heard about dating?

I've heard people say to not date, but start with engagement in a way – to commit straight away. I mean, in a way it is true... I wouldn't start dating someone if I didn't think that I would end up marrying that person, so in some ways I can understand that. I would certainly stop dating someone if I thought there was no way it would lead to marriage. I don't want to spend time and energy and invest in someone if I can better use that energy in other areas of my life – I've always been very practical in that way!

But I also think there needs to be a freedom, especially at the start of a relationship. You do need to try and you do need that time to really get to know each other, but bearing in mind that he might become my husband or she might become my wife. I think that exploration time is really healthy, but I think if you just date for the sake of it, I think that's a different thing. I wouldn't do that because there is a lot of heartache involved.

But there is also a lot of heartache involved if you commit too quickly before you've had chance to find out if it is the right relationship for you. I wouldn't wait too long, either – I think if you know that it is right...

Many people have a fear of commitment, and young men especially have a fear of commitment, and the only way to break it is to just do it.

So I do think it is healthy that at some point you need to go for it, but I do think there is a time and a space for dating as well... rather than to commit on the first day.

But it's very different for everyone. God really doesn't work in just one way. There are so many stories you know of people who got engaged after just one month and that was good for them. For me it took almost two years of dating...

So tell me how you met your husband, then?

I fell in love with Maarten twice. First of all when I was twenty-six but then I found out he was twenty-one years older than me and I thought, 'It's not possible.' I was in love with him for about four months but I never talked with him about it. I never brought it up. We were just friends. God did speak to me a little bit at that time from the book of Ruth, with her relationship with Boaz, but it didn't happen. Later I looked back and I could see that it was God speaking to me, but I was waiting for the fulfilment right then!

Then, of course, Maarten made a decision to go to the UK (we were living in New Zealand) and then I thought, 'I've got my answer.' We stayed in contact a bit – we read each other's newsletters, but that was about it.

Then I came to England in October 2011. When he read in my newsletter that I was coming, he emailed, 'I live in London, do you want to catch up for a coffee?' and so I visited him in London. It was nice, but I realised I didn't have any romantic feelings for him anymore.

The next time I was in London with friends we met up again, and it was after that I realised I actually still liked him. I was so annoyed at myself! That chapter was over, the book was closed!

But then I had a good chat with my sister and a close friend. They said something interesting that made me think. They said, 'If, after six years you both are still single, and you still have feelings for him, maybe you should do something with it.' So after a long conversation and prayer that night, I felt a peace and wrote Maarten an email the next day and told him how I felt.

I said, 'Hey, I like you, I do have feelings for you, we have never talked about it. I have no idea if you have some feelings for me, but if you want to come to my home in Holland for Boxing Day [in three days' time!) you are very welcome.'

And he came! By New Year's Eve, my heart was already for Maarten.

We dated for almost two years and just before we got engaged I felt God say that the time of waiting was over. I think that you can actually get comfortable in the waiting. I was actually afraid and I was frustrated and I wanted to get married and I felt God say, 'The time of waiting is over, you have to move forward now' and although waiting is frustrating I found myself thinking, 'I don't know if I want to take the next step and move forward.' I didn't expect to feel like that.

So this is part of Esther's wedding speech that she read on her wedding day:

> In my single years I learned to love Jesus as the lover of my soul and my husband-maker and I found the deep fulfilment of love and safety that I can only find in Him. To such an extent that I wasn't afraid to stay single the rest of my life. But I still believed God had a man for me so I prayed that He would lead me into a marriage. Today I stepped over the line and walk into His fulfilled promises. James 1:17 says: 'Every good gift and every perfect gift is from above, and comes down from the Father of lights, with whom there is no variation or shadow of turning.'
>
> From our first week of dating, we had a sense of being God's good and perfect gift for one another.
>
> I've seen the faithfulness of God in these two years of what has sometimes been a rocky relationship, so that whatever happens, His plans are bigger and further-reaching than only ourselves and more is yet to come.

Now you are six months' married, how do you feel about your single years?

First of all, my relationship with God has only got stronger through my marriage because I so need God! Marriage is like a mirror and I realise I am no better than anyone else and am so in need of the grace of God!

But honestly, I'm so happy with that foundation that I have in God. It is so, so, so life-giving for my marriage. I think it is really helpful and useful to work through things in your life before you get married. To face difficulties or to get disciplined in certain areas of your life to get control, if you have a problem with eating or a problem with something else.

I think that is a gift you can give to your husband or your wife.

To find that love and safety first and foremost in God, instead of in your husband, is so healthy and it's good if you find your husband feels that way too. I really learned during those single years not to expect certain things from your husband that only God can give. The deep fulfilment and the deep joy and the deep, deep fullness of life can only be found in Him, and I think that releases your husband a little bit in your marriage. When he knows that you do not put that on him; yes, there is that part that your husband does fulfil but God, You are my joy and You are life!

Finally, was there a particular turning point in your relationship with God that brought peace in those single years?

Yes. I was in Spain on a Leadership Development Course in 2010 run by YWAM and I had – it sounds a bit funny – an encounter with God that was a bit like a marriage. It was on my first or second night that I kind of had a bit of a vision... a picture... I saw a box, and the box was my heart and something was stuck in my heart and still needed to be unlocked. I didn't know what it was, but then I felt like God said, 'I know you gave your heart to Me, but I also give My heart to you.'

It just hit me in a new way that I never thought about before. It felt a bit like a covenant relationship where I said to God 'I do' – I do give my heart to You and in return, He said, 'I say the same to you.'

After that first night, my time in Spain was like a honeymoon. I really felt God, kind of, romancing me, in a way. But I also think that

God brought me to that place. I couldn't make it happen, it came spontaneously. The Holy Spirit led me at a certain time. It was a really intimate time which has been quite significant for me. I feel now that I follow God out of a real heart-to-heart love relationship with Him. It's a passion; to love Him, and Him loving me.

Emma's story

Emma is a single, stunning young woman in her mid-thirties with a gentle and deeply compassionate heart, and she loves to laugh. She was raised on a farm in New Zealand, is now a nurse, and we once discovered, to her enormous delight, that apparently, she has the same temperament as Anne of Green Gables!

Emma, would you mind sharing some of the struggles you've had with being single?

I've always had the desire to be married and it waxes and wanes at times. At the times of waning it is quite freeing, as life is really good being single. There are the freedoms you don't have when you are in a marriage partnership – which I think we all know about.

Sometimes, especially as I get past the point where I thought I would be married, there are other emotions and realities to deal with. Sometimes these catch me off guard – at a time when I'm not thinking about marriage or kids. For example, as a nurse I was reading a list of the women coming in for elective caesarean sections. I noticed that the year of one women's birth was the same as mine. She was having a baby and I wasn't even in a relationship. I just felt like someone kicked me in the heart... and then I carried on working.

Sometimes I wonder if it's my fault I'm single. Am I too fussy? Am I not focusing on God enough? Has marriage become an idol? And I lay it down repeatedly... hoping God will then give me the desire of my heart. When He doesn't, I try again as I figure perhaps I didn't do it properly and I am still idolatrous!

Have you ever had any bad relationship experiences?

Yes, I've had abusive relationships. In one relationship, when I was quite young, my boyfriend would try to coerce me into sex using emotional manipulation. He would come to church – even got baptised – and then abused me verbally, and the church. He was quite controlling. He would smoke marijuana and then say if I was really a Christian I would forgive him and take him back…. I ended that one!

What do you want from a man?

Someone kind and Christian and dependable. I had 'a list' earlier of some ridiculous things also!

Would you say you have given your heart fully to Jesus in this area of looking for love?

It's definitely a struggle. I've had a few 'consecration ceremonies' over the years. Nowadays it's more like God says 'don't give up hope' and I say, 'It's OK, God, it's not your fault. I'm fine, it's OK.'

It can be hard to know where the lines of responsibility lie at times, especially in Christian culture. It ranges from the more passive – 'Just wait and honour God and He will bring the right man along' – to Christian books that give advice on where to hang out to meet men. I think the most damaging aspect of Christian culture for me personally has been the feeling of failure. I don't want to come across as a victim as people are more than well-meaning, but sometimes the repeated refrains of 'seek ye first and God will give you the desires of your heart' (two scriptures I just welded together!) applied to relationships gets a bit old. Someone such as myself who you might say has experienced 'protracted singleness' can then equate this to…

'I'm a sucky Christian. I desire marriage but I haven't managed to get there, so I must be not seeking God enough. Not godly enough. A failure.'

I realise this sounds a bit defeatist, but I know other women feel the same. It doesn't help when the newly-marrieds or engaged couples repeat the refrain and you think... yes! See, they know it. It proves it. I am failing somehow. But there are some good blogs out there (like fast.pray.)[1] that I've found really helpful.

What lessons would you say God has been teaching you during your single years?

First of all, He has encouraged me to 'cast out my net' and still have hope when I'd rather curl up and protect my heart.

But most of all, when the pain is intense and you think God doesn't care or understand, He does. He sees, He hears and He understands. I was amazed with the scriptures He gave me.

Like once, after a particularly painful break-up (the lose 5kg, can't stop crying, can't eat kind of break-up), I was by myself, upset, despairing and hurt. I felt a surge of anger and despair towards God – that He didn't understand my pain. How could He get what it is like to be a twenty-nine-year-old woman in today's world? There were more issues of world importance He had to deal with, I was sure.

I was met with a swift revelation of three Bible verses that left me in no doubt of His care and understanding. The first was reading about Hagar [Hagar was servant to Sarah, who persuaded her husband, Abraham, to conceive a child with Hagar. When Hagar was pregnant she was mistreated by Sarah and ran away.] Hagar was wandering in the desert when God found her. He redirected and reassured her. I felt like I was wandering in the desert of despair regarding the end of this relationship, and God didn't really care or couldn't understand the struggles of my heart. What stuck out to me was her response: 'You are the God who sees me' [see Genesis 16:13]. Me, just me, truly me – He sees me and understands my circumstances. I felt I could identify with her.

The next verse was Psalm 18:6: 'In my distress [when seemingly closed in] I called upon the Lord and cried to my God; He heard my voice out of His temple (heavenly dwelling place), and my cry came before Him, into His [very] ears' (AMP Classic). This personalised to me how much He really heard my cry. If a noise really goes into your very ears – you can't avoid it! It's not a background noise, it's not a mumble or an unnoticed voice, He really hears it. As well as hearing it, He reassured me with the next verses. (He wanted me to be in no doubt!)

The next verses were Isaiah 40:27–28: 'Why do you complain, Jacob, Why do you say, Israel, 'My way is hidden from the LORD; my cause is disregarded by my God'? Do you not know? Have you not heard? The LORD is the everlasting God, the Creator of the ends of the earth. He will not grow tired or weary, and his understanding no one can fathom.' As we know, this chapter then leads on to giving hope for the future.

Wow, I was overcome. He really does understand how hard it is for us at times. We are not alone in our struggles.

What would you say to a young woman who is in the same shoes as you were ten years ago?

I would say… You're gorgeous and talented. You have a gift to give to the world that nobody else can. If you desire marriage it is not a bad thing, but life doesn't always proceed as we plan. If your man doesn't turn up 'on time', it is not a reflection of your worth or of your level of obedience. It's just life. Perhaps there are reasons for the delay, and look into that too. Work on your junk! Pray. Ask God. But don't fall into the trap of believing that marriage is a reward for good behaviour or faithfulness to God. And if you find your man or he finds you – yay!

Don't give up but don't waste your life waiting for a man to complete you. Live the life you love and if he arrives, it's a bonus.

Gosh, that sounds clichéd!

Let's not end on a cliché

Esther, Emma and I once had lives that were fairly similar. We all worked for YWAM Marine Reach, based in the same office in New Zealand. We would fly back and forth to Fiji to work with medical mission teams on board our medical ship the MV *Pacific Link*. That all changed when I stopped flying on mission and started having babies. Esther and Emma continued flying off to Fiji and Samoa, and Esther even flew to the UK and Albania to develop a Europe office and then flew to Spain for a leadership training school for six weeks. She became medical director, in charge of multiple teams across the globe at the same time as I decided to stop work to become a full-time mum. I had a moment of 'Mummy blues' when I compared her life to mine – she was doing all the things I'd dreamed of doing and here I was stuck at home on the sofa! But then I remembered how much Esther longed to be in my shoes. I knew her longing to be a wife and mother was just as strong as my desire to travel and make the world a better place.

My point is that comparison to other people's lives doesn't lead to happiness. We can find comfort in lives that are similar to ours and we can be inspired by those whose lives we admire, but ultimately, as Theodore Roosevelt said, 'Comparison is the thief of joy.' However much you envy some aspects of another person's life, there will certainly be someone looking at you and envying some aspects of yours.

Chapter Twelve
Dealing with the Unexpected

For the rest of you who are in mixed marriages – Christian married to non-Christian – we have no explicit command from the Master. So this is what you must do. If you are a man with a wife who is not a believer but who still wants to live with you, hold on to her. If you are a woman with a husband who is not a believer but he wants to live with you, hold on to him ... On the other hand, if the unbelieving spouse walks out, you've got to let him or her go. You don't have to hold on desperately. God has called us to make the best of it, as peacefully as we can.
(1 Corinthians 7:12–16, *The Message*)

When I was pregnant with my first child, I went to a class that taught us 'what to expect' for childbirth. Ideally, we would all have smooth, natural labours and end up with a perfectly healthy baby who would immediately fall into a perfect feeding and sleeping pattern. The class glossed over things like caesareans or bottle feeding, perhaps in the belief that if we believe for the best, that's what we'll get. In reality, while many of us in the group did experience normal labour and healthy babies, we also had our fair share of caesareans, prolonged labours and one super-fast labour that almost resulted in the baby being born in the car on the way to the hospital. While we had been prepared for the expected, we were not prepared for the unexpected! The reality is that we are all a work-in-progress, still being prepared to be the bride of Christ and some things don't go as smoothly as we would like.

Paul, in 1 Corinthians 7, recognises that not everything in a marriage goes as we would expect and he offers advice for this, reminding us that above all things we are called to live in peace with one another. I love the way *The Message* puts it: 'God has called us to make the best of it, as peacefully as we can.'

Lisa's story

Lisa[1] is a wonderful, lovely young woman. She went to an all-girls' high school and to church and youth group on the weekend. In the summer, she went to Soul Survivor with her youth group just like many thousands of other young people in the UK, and – like many of us dream of – she met and fell in love with a boy from church when she was just eighteen and they married four years later. Four years into their marriage, they were expecting their first child when things began to change. Her husband, Andy, began to share with Lisa significant doubts he had been having about their shared Christian faith. This is Lisa's story of grace when dealing with the unexpected. Even though she didn't plan for her marriage to take this turn, God still prepared her for it.

Lisa, how long have you been married?

This year we will have been married for eight years. Eight years, two children and two rabbits.

What are some of the highlights over those eight years?

The wedding day. That sounds obvious, but it was such an amazing day and I look back on it with an huge amount of thankfulness and joy.

What made it so wonderful?

Well, marrying Andy! That was the main thing. I think it was just such a nice celebration. I remember walking down the aisle and seeing Andy – and seeing rows and rows of faces that I loved, people who were there for us and supporting us, was just great. I love people, so having a day when you are surrounded by those who love you and want the best for you was just the greatest feeling in the world.

How God-centred was your ceremony?

We were aware that lots of people were coming to our wedding who didn't normally attend church so wanted to make sure it was as God-focused yet inclusive as possible. The worship was very special, as were the Bible readings and talk, but all in all, I think it was just a joyful day with a lot of God's goodness mixed in to all the fun and festivities.

Other highlights would be...

Lots of things! We've had a lot of fun together, and a lot of really special times. Andy is the person that I know the best, but also the person I want to know me the best. He's the person I enjoy hanging out with the most. We didn't live together so that meant that there was a lot of newness when we got married. Everything was just different, which was really exciting and really good fun.

And more recently we've had highlights like moving into our new house and bringing our children into the world. That's easily the biggest highlight – seeing Andy as a dad has been a new way of falling in love with him.

So when you first got married, was your faith a part of your relationship?

Growing up in the same church youth group as each other, faith was obviously a dynamic of our relationship from the outset, and although there's lots of ways in which we weren't typical – we rarely had quiet times together, for instance – we would talk about significant things in the context of faith and pray for changes and breakthroughs and healings and that kind of thing. And we were both very motivated by social action (like helping lead the youth group together, and charity work), so many practical things we did were out of a flow of 'this is what we believe'.

When did you begin to notice any change?

I think our differences in faith started to come up about four years into our marriage. I guess I'd felt like Andy had been a little more disengaged with things and in the summer of 2012 he said, 'I'm not really sure about this anymore.'

What did he mean?

It was his way of putting it – quite tentative and kind and not very confrontational. What then emerged was that he had been on a journey of doubting lots of aspects of faith for a little while.

What did that feel like for you?

Um. It was sort of, devastating, really. In lots of ways. Because... it was sort of like... I guess having the rug pulled from beneath your feet. Looking back, I can recall times when I felt 'Andy's not really on board with this', but I'd never really joined the dots so it felt like a big surprise. It was hard because I didn't know what to do with that. It felt like uncharted territory. From my early teens I had thought, it's best to date a Christian, it's best to marry a Christian, and I had done those things – I'm not saying that I expected God would never give me a hard time! But I had actually made those choices and done those things based on the thought that the Christian element was set in stone. So it basically shook my world and shook my way of thinking about how it would all play out. And I think I felt quite alone. For a while at least.

Did that have any knock-on effects in your marriage?

As soon as it was clear that Andy was having – at the time – quite significant doubts, it raised questions to me about our foundations, as it were. I remember feeling quite worried about that for a while. Thinking, what if we can't agree on things anymore? And what if we think differently about things, and what about church? And we're about to have our first child, and how does that all work in terms of raising them in faith or not in faith? If I look back on this list, I would say that we haven't resolved about 95 per cent of these things. I don't have an answer for them, but I no longer worry about them, either, if that makes sense.

Can you give me an example?

A big one was the idea of how to raise our children. Raising children within the church and within the faith was something I was very concerned about immediately because it just wasn't a route I'd imagined navigating. The idea of actually working all that out with a child when it's not necessarily what you both believe. And, like I say, I don't think we've ever resolved that, but I don't worry about it so much anymore. I feel very thankful that Andy is still happy to come along to church, so we take our kids to church. We dedicated them rather than baptised them as babies (our church catered for both). Andy was happy to say that he was thankful for them but to say 'I stand against the devil' was probably a bit much for him. And that was fine by me.

Do Andy's doubts ever shake your faith?

No. I wouldn't say they have. I mean, I wouldn't now say that nothing will ever shake my faith because I know that things can and do. But it didn't make me question God. I guess what it's done is change my faith, in a positive way mostly, in that it has opened my eyes to a lot of different perspectives. I now don't feel worried about raising children in a family where there is doubt and uncertainty about faith because I think: Well, that's life! The process of figuring out what they think would need to happen anyway. So I no longer think it's a bad thing for them to have that freedom to ask questions in the safe environment of a family. Saying all that they're still only little, so ask me in ten years' time – I may have a different answer!

How has your perspective on marriage and faith changed?

I no longer see faith as a given, I see it as a relationship. I believe God is constant, but we change all the time and so that means we need to show honesty and flexibility in the way we develop that relationship. In the same way, marriage is a relationship which is immensely life-giving, but if you want the best from it, you don't assume that 'well, we are married now so it is all going to be fine' and just do nothing to maintain or deepen it! There will always be things that surprise you or come to shake up your marriage.

Has this turn of events changed the way you expected your life to go?

There are things which we previously would have done or ministries we might have led and that can feel hard because I'm quite an impatient person! But on the other hand, it has deepened my faith considerably. Now I have empathy for, and have become more accessible to, people who are on the edge of faith in a way that I don't think I had before. Andy is not someone who is against everything Christianity stands for – and I do know people for whom that has been the case – so I'm thankful for that.

Have there been times that you have looked at another marriage and felt envious?

Yeah, something I had to fight against was idolising the perfect Christian marriage – especially in the earlier days when we were really trying to figure things out – but I know that when you scratch beneath the surface, no one's marriage is perfect.

Can something good, like marriage, be an idol?

The Bible verse that has spoken to me at various times including early on in our marriage is in the book of Jonah when he was inside the fish. Jonah says something like: 'Those who cling to worthless idols forfeit the grace that could be theirs.'[2] That is something that

God has spoken to me about on a number of different issues from money, to careers and the obvious idols-type things, right through to marriage itself. And I do think – this is where I could get on my soapbox – one of the really interesting challenges for the Church is to uphold the idea of marriage and to celebrate marriage, but also to not let marriage become an idol – that is, for the idea of it to not replace God. It's important to try not to convey the idea of marriage as being perfect and therefore either unattainable if you are single, or if you are married and it's not a perfect marriage, therefore you've failed.

God is good, because He already had been teaching me about having grace for ourselves in our marriage (I was prompted to read *What's so Amazing about Grace?* by Philip Yancey[3] just before Andy and I had that initial conversation, and that was very helpful!). Having grace for when it's not perfect, and having grace when it's not what you thought it was going to be, and having grace for each other and for other people. I need to have grace for Andy because I can't force him into being this Christian husband that ticks all the boxes – he's not that, no one is!

What is marriage all about, then?

I THINK BEING MARRIED IS AN INCREDIBLE OPPORTUNITY TO LEARN HOW TO LOVE AND BE LOVED.

It is a constant process of discipleship, of becoming less about myself and more about us (and then it all changes again with kids...!) Like you say in your book about being tested in the fire – it's not easy and it's not without cost or sacrifice. So it is really important that your wedding day is a day of celebration and anticipation, because actually the ins and outs of becoming one with someone else who thinks differently to you and who may think differently to you in ways you don't even know, and may never fully know or understand, is a complex and refining process.

So four years after this life-changing conversation, what does your marriage look like?

Andy is the person that I love most in the world and actually, once I got past my little cloud of worries and accepted that this was what things were going to look like for us, whatever the length of this season, I wanted to concentrate on empathising with him – this was actually a really scary and troubling time for Andy. I needed to be there for him and to be supportive and not pressurising. So now we process things a bit differently, but we are definitely better at listening and learning from each other and from other people than when it all began!

Would you still encourage Christian girls to marry Christian boys, or are you tempted to think: 'What's the point?'

It is tempting to think 'What's the point?' but I don't believe that. I think our faith is what grounds us and shapes us so it is a good thing to look for someone who is also seeking to be grounded and shaped by the same set of beliefs. I just think investing in your faith is the best thing you can do, for you and for anyone you might marry.

What I would say, actually, is that I think character is important. It's not just enough to say that you believe something. How do you behave? Something that I am thankful for is my husband's strong and kind character, which hasn't changed despite the differences now in what he would say he believes or doesn't believe.

So, let's say you could meet your younger self. What advice would you give?

Firstly, invest in your relationship with God and with other people, not just a boyfriend. Seeking to have strong foundations in faith is something that we can all do.

Also, enjoy the independence of singleness. There are lots of benefits to life before marriage so don't idolise marriage. This might sound odd coming from me, a person who married at twenty-two, but one of things I valued about having a long-distance relationship was that I got to do a lot of things that had I got married at eighteen, wouldn't have happened in the same way. So take the opportunities and enjoy the freedom that life brings.

And try to be someone who has grace for yourself and grace for other people, be that your husband or whoever. I think being kind to ourselves is really important. There's a quote which I like which goes something like, 'Be kind, everyone you meet is fighting a battle' and I think it's true of our inner battles as much as for our conduct with other people!

Get real with God

What's been your journey of looking for love so far?

Is there anything from Esther's story that encourages or challenges you?

Is there anything from Emma's story that stands out to you?

Is there anything from Lisa's story that you want to remember?

Part Four:
Be Found:
You and Your Relationship with God

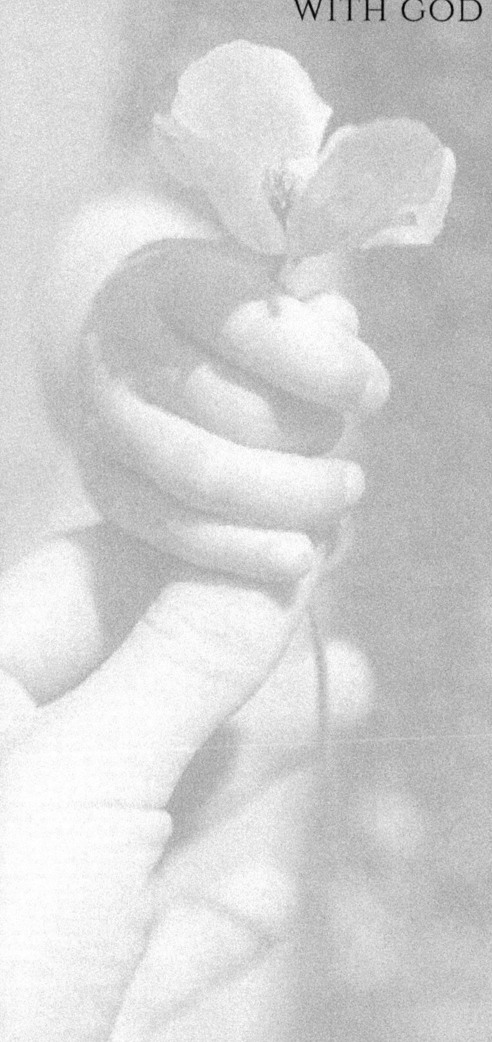

Chapter Thirteen
Jesus Christ: Lord, Friend and Lover

I am my beloved's,
And his desire is towards me.
(Song of Solomon 7:10)

The Father and the Son and the Holy Spirit have a relationship with each other; one so harmonious that they are one: one God.

One of the beautiful things about the Trinity – Father, Son and Holy Spirit – is that they are all about relationship. When people try to explain the Trinity in abstract terms, I find it confusing. When they try to explain it in concrete terms, like the ice/water/steam analogy or the sun/ray/warmth one, I find it interesting, but a little bit irrelevant. When I think of the Trinity in terms of relationship, I don't need to constantly define God, I can actually meet Him and enjoy Him in all of the many, many wonderful ways He has given us. Father, friend, helper, teacher, provider, healer, comforter, shepherd, priest, refiner, judge, Saviour, bridegroom... the list goes on and on.

What do you notice about all of those names and titles that are given to God in the Bible? What stands out to me is that they are all definitions in terms of relationship – they all describe one aspect of how we can relate to God. The only one that doesn't is Yahweh – 'the I Am'. The name God told Moses was His own (Exodus 3:14). This one shows us that God is utterly complete and whole apart from us – He doesn't need us to help Him satisfy His identity. But...

All His other names help us understand our identity.

And when we can understand that, everything else falls into place. Does that make sense? To help understand this, let's look briefly at three of these names, Jesus is Lord, Jesus is friend and Jesus is bridegroom.

Jesus, your Lord

At some point in our relationship with God, we approach Jesus as Lord. What does this tell us about our identity? It's tells us that we are not God. God is God and we are not. Unless we admit that to ourselves and to Him, we are always battling with God for the driving seat in our own lives. If you look back at Adam and Eve, you can see the motivation that led them to sin was the idea that they could be like God – it wasn't enough to be made in His image and given dominion over the earth, they were arrogant enough to believe that they could play a role only God is qualified for.

It is foundational to our faith to humble ourselves, acknowledge that our way is not the best way and hand over our lives to the one who knows and loves us best and who has bought us with His blood: Jesus. At this point, it is a master/servant relationship, one of submitting our lives, our rights and our eternity to our Creator who loves us and died for us. This relationship is foundational, it is essential and we often come back to this kind of relationship with God at different times in our lives, but it is not the end of the relationship's journey.

Jesus talks about different levels of relationship. Shortly before He died, there is a very beautiful moment when He touchingly tells His disciples that He is no longer just their master, but that they may call Him their friend. He has allowed them to enter into a deeper level of understanding of the things of God, a level that only a friend may enter (John 15:15).

Jesus, your friend

In our own relationship with Jesus, we often get to know Him as our friend. Some think this is a flippant description of our relationship with God but actually, the friend relationship is a very privileged one. Moses and Abraham, two giants of faith in the Old Testament are described as being Friends with God (Exodus 33:11; 2 Chronicles 20:7; James 2:23). Jesus called His disciples His friends (Matthew 9:15, Luke 12:4) and was described by others as being a friend of sinners (Matthew 11:19). Jesus Himself put a high price on friendship when He said, 'Greater love has no one than this, than to lay down one's life for his friends' (John 15:13).

A FRIENDSHIP WITH JESUS IS A BEAUTIFUL AND WONDERFUL THING TO ENJOY.

To call ourselves a Christian is to have the privilege of calling ourselves 'Jesus' friend'. Just like Moses and Abraham, like Peter and James and John. Jesus died for you, because He was your friend. And it is the friends of Jesus who are entrusted with the work of His kingdom here on earth.[1] Wow.

Jesus, your bridegroom

Have you ever read a love story or watched a movie in which a girl is looking for Mr Perfect-for-her and she has a best friend of the opposite sex who she talks to about it? As the story develops, she realises that Mr Perfect-for-her has been there all along in the guise of her best friend, only she didn't realise it. The 1989 movie *When Harry Met Sally* with Billy Crystal and Meg Ryan is a famous one. There are others like *13 going on 30* (2004) or *Valentine's Day* (2010) with Ashton Kutcher and Jennifer Garner's characters falling in love after years of being best friends. It's a theme as old as Jane Austin's heroine *Emma* (1815) and Lucy Maud Montgomery's Anne Shirley and Gilbert Blythe from *Anne of Green Gables* (1908). Can you tell I like a good love story?

Jesus calls Himself many titles and one of them is bridegroom. We, the Church, also have many titles and one of them is the bride of Christ.

PART OF YOUR NEW IDENTITY WHEN YOU BECOME BORN AGAIN, IS THAT YOU ARE THE BRIDE OF CHRIST...

...being prepared for a very special day.[2] This is a different relationship to that of friend, but it is not one that comes quickly or easily. Like any relationship, it takes time to develop trust and intimacy with Jesus. And Jesus knows this so I don't believe He's in a hurry. He's the friend who will walk with you and by you until hopefully, one day, you may realise that He is also the lover who has been there all along.

To be honest, I haven't always been comfortable with the idea of Jesus as lover of my soul. Jesus only began to reveal Himself to me as bridegroom *after* I was married. I was doing a Discipleship Training School (DTS) on a YWAM Ship[3] in New Zealand listening to a woman teach about hearing God's voice. After the teaching session we were given a chance to practise – to pray, to listen and to write what we thought God was saying to us in that moment. The question I asked God was: 'What do You think and feel about me?' What I wrote was too personal to share but from that moment, Jesus the lover walked into my life and my intimacy with Him deepened to a whole new level. At first I was unsure about seeing Jesus in this new light – was it really Him? Was I being deceived? But as I began to explore the Bible, I saw him emerging from the pages in a way I had never seen before.

Ephesians 5:29 that says that Jesus nourishes us and cherishes us, just like a person would their own body. 1 Corinthians 6:17 says, just as a man and a woman become one, through sexual union, that 'he who is joined to the Lord is one spirit with Him'. In Hosea

2:14–16 God speaks of the people of Judah so: "I will allure her, will bring her into the wilderness, And speak comfort to her… [she] will call Me "My Husband,' and no longer call Me "My Master …"'

Then there's the Old Testament book of the Song of Solomon (or Song of Songs) that is devoted to the intimacy of lovers, mirroring our unfolding, growing relationship with Jesus Christ. The Amplified Bible introduces the Song of Solomon with this note: 'Among the multitudes who read the Bible there are comparatively few who have a clear understanding of the Song of Solomon.' It then goes on to explain that it is more like a drama than a poem whose parts are not obviously assigned without some knowledge of the original language. So it is a book that cannot be understood simply by reading, but must be brought alive. Imagine it more like a Greek drama that is sung, not spoken, and accompanied by actors acting out the relationship between a bridegroom and a lover.

Its language is incredibly passionate, full of rich metaphors and overwhelming outbursts of love and worship and adoration from both bride and bridegroom towards each other. His love and affection for her are not reserved like a British gentleman might show towards his demure wife, with a peck on the cheek or a pat on the head. No, they hold absolutely nothing back in their display of love and adoration and passion. This is the bridegroom speaking to his bride: 'Behold, you are fair, my love! Behold, you are fair!' (1:15). 'You have ravished my heart, my sister, my spouse; you have ravished my heart with one look of your eyes … How much better than wine is your love' (4:9–10). And the woman uses such phrases as: 'My beloved is white and ruddy, chief among ten thousand. His head is like the finest gold; his locks are wavy, and black as a raven … His mouth is most sweet, Yes, he is altogether lovely. This is my beloved, and this is my friend …' (5:10–16).

The bridegroom feasts on her love. She invites him – 'Let my beloved come to his garden And eat its pleasant fruits' (4:16) – her love is a source of joy to him and he is not afraid to display it to the whole world with banners of praise and love: 'He brought me to the banqueting house, and his banner over me was love' (2:4).

However, the truly beautiful moments are not in public but in private. In the beginning of our walk with the Lord and regularly throughout it, Jesus draws us into private places of intimacy where we can spend time just being with our Lord. 'I ... brought him to the house of my mother ... into the chamber of her who conceived me' (3:4). These are close, intimate times of communion with our Lord. Not asking for anything, not coming to require help, but spending time together, just because.

How do you feel about this kind of romantic, indulgent, expressive, emotional language spoken over you? You. *You*. All for you. The woman in the beginning of the drama can't help but notice her own lack of worthiness in the presence of one so majestic. She describes herself as dark, tanned, stained and ruined by her time spent in the world (1:5–6). But the beloved calls her lovely.[4] She describes herself as a 'rose of Sharon' or a 'lily of the valleys' (2:1) – a common flower, scentless, lowly, nothing particularly special about her. The bridegroom replies that while she may be a lowly flower, she is a 'lily among thorns' (2:2).

You and I may just be like plain, everyday, lowly flowers and wonder why in the world Jesus would be so enraptured with us. And He would reply that yes, we are simply flowers, but He has chosen us. He has plucked us out from among the thorns and, plain and lowly as we may be, He loves us and has chosen to wear us on His breast for all the world to see.

As we spend more time with Christ, making Him the focus of our thoughts, our time, our objectives in life, we become more like Him, like the gold refined in the fire, and when He looks at us He can confidently say, 'You are all fair, my love, And there is no spot in you' (4:7).

Have you ever looked at the face of someone who is so enveloped in worship with Jesus that they are unaware of anything else –

their face tilted upwards, body at rest in His presence? The face of such a person is beautiful. Even the plainest or most scarred face in the world is transformed when in this state of adoration towards Jesus. I've seen it and it is heart-melting. That's what Jesus sees when our attention is solely on Him. That is the place where He finds joy and feasts in His garden of fruit! This place of worship, of wholehearted adoration, is just for Him and Him alone – a garden shut up to everyone else but Him (4:12). This is the attitude of heart, mind and body that He is longing for and searching for and wooing you for. Have you ever given that to Him? Your everything? He loves you.

He loves you, oh precious daughter of the King, He loves you!

When the Bible describes God as jealous (Exodus 34:14) it is not as the angry Zeus might be jealous of a competitive suitor and will throw cruel lightning bolts to get them out of the way. No. He is as a lover, jealous for this time with you, for this place of one-on-one, private intimacy with you. He's jealous for your time, your affection. Why? Because He loves you! He died for you! He came from heaven to earth for you, sacrificed Himself because He so loves to be with you! He loves you.

This is the wonderful, transformational reality of a relationship with God – that our needs were made to be met. That they cannot be fully and completely met by each other does not mean we need to supress them or live a life of disappointment – no! We can turn to God, our Maker and our Source. And what is God's answer to the need for affectionate, nourishing love to our souls? He sent the most perfect, loving man who ever lived to sweep us off our feet. A man who loves us more deeply and passionately than anyone else ever could. A man who is so committed to loving us that He gave

His life for us. God sent His Son. God, our Father, the source of all love, sent us Jesus.

Get real with God

On the next page is a Blob Diagram. It's just a picture with Blob people that you can use to help you think about your relationship with God. There are no labels on the people and no interpretation for what each one is doing. Look at the picture and think about which Blobs best describe you and Jesus right now (or add your own). Your interpretation of what two of the Blobs are doing might be different to someone else's interpretation, and that is fine. After you've decided which Blobs best describe you and Jesus, write a sentence to describe in words what you see in the picture.

Which Blob is you? Which Blob is Jesus? Why?

This Blob Diagram, and others made by Blobtree, can be a useful thing to hold on to, so feel free to bookmark that page. You can come back to it at different times of your life – even different times of the day! – to help you understand and unpack your changing relationship with God. Perhaps God will use it to show you or teach you something.

BLOB RELATIONSHIP
© IAN LONG + PIP WILSON 2014
www.blobtree.com

Chapter Fourteen
Our Father, In Heaven

Your Father knows what you need
before you ask him.
(Matthew 6:8, NIV UK 2011)

As uncomfortable as I was when Jesus first began to reveal Himself through the Scriptures as lover, it was a concept I connected with well. I could relate to that, having wanted a lover my entire life. What has been even more difficult for me is to get to know God as my Father. I have been happy to accept the idea, the concept of a heavenly Father, but the reality of it in my life has been fairly nominal. God was my Father, yes, but did I have a father-daughter relationship with Him? A year ago I would have said yes, but I would have been fooling myself.

I REALLY, REALLY DIDN'T WANT TO WRITE THIS CHAPTER.

It wasn't in my first twenty-six drafts of this book. In fact, other books I've read about young women with 'father wounds' have always made me gag a little because I find them cringeworthy. Why? Maybe because I didn't believe I needed to hear it. So if this 'Father's love' stuff makes you want to skim through this chapter and get onto something that can 'really help you', then I very much understand how you feel. But please don't. Because it could be that, like me, God wants to show you something.

The love of an earthly father is supposed to be our introduction to the love of our heavenly Father. Sometimes our earthly father, who God intended to love us, wasn't there for us or didn't love us the way he should have and without realising, unless we have taken deliberate steps not to, we naturally assume God is like our earthly dad. So your relationship, or lack of relationship with your human dad – as much as you might not like to hear this – has a direct impact on your relationship with your heavenly one. Well, of course it has! Your heavenly Father is invisible so what else have you got to base your experience of fatherhood on? We can read all about Jesus' relationship with His Father and think 'That's nice for Him' and we can see others with seemingly perfect relationships with their dads and think 'That's nice for them' and convince ourselves that since it is theoretically possible to have a great relationship with a father, then you can theoretically have a great one with God. But it's that head and heart thing all over again. I know God is a good Father – I know it in my head. Why don't I know it in my heart?

Some dads are good dads who meet all your needs as best they can. I have always considered this to be my dad. Then there are absent dads whom you've never met, disapproving dads you can never seem to please, abusive dads who cause all kinds of emotional as well as physical trauma, and then there's the passive dad. The dad who is there but not there. When I first heard someone describe this kind of dad, it rang a bell. Slowly, I realised that in my relationship with my dad, there was a connection missing somewhere.

I love my dad and he is, on the whole, a decent guy. He has his flaws but he has always been there for me and provided for me. He is not particularly disapproving and has never been cruel or unkind. I've never gone without – all of my physical needs have always been met. That makes a good dad, right? Yes, that definitely makes a good dad. But it doesn't make a perfect dad. None of us have one of those, I'm afraid.

Pastor Jimmy Evans from Texas, USA, has a really helpful way of explaining what makes a perfect Father. He summarises five basic needs that we all have, that a father is supposed to fill. They are:

protection, provision, nurture/affection, training (as in, modelling lifestyle) and guidance (as in personal guidance).

THE PERFECT FATHER PROVIDES ALL THESE AND GOD IS A PERFECT FATHER.

ꟷ

If you doubt that, Pastor Jimmy Evans' advice is to 'Trust God as if He's the perfect Father until He proves you wrong'.[1] I like that!

My dad was excellent at meeting the 'provision need'. I've always had a place to live, food to eat and a generous allowance. He paid my way through university and even as an adult working as a volunteer missionary, his first question is always: 'Is there anything you need?' As a result, I have rarely had a problem believing that God is my provider and will provide for all my physical needs. I can certainly thank my dad, with all my heart, for teaching me that.

Dad was pretty good at meeting the protection need too – even if, as a teenager, I resented being picked up first from every school disco or him driving around the streets looking for me if I wasn't home by 7pm. But then I've never been seriously hurt in my life, either, so thanks, Dad.

Dad modelled to me some things, like having a strong work ethic, being a committed member of the local church, eating together as a family, and the importance of tithing, and I got snippets of personal guidance here and there. But when it came to nurture and affection... that was something that did not come naturally to my dad. I think he left all that kind of stuff up to Mum. (Who did an outstanding job, by the way. Thank you, Mum). To be fair, that was the culture he was raised in – mums stayed at home and nurtured, dads went out and worked.

Not that Dad didn't love me, but we rarely hug or kiss or cuddle or say, 'I love you.' It feels very awkward when we do. He was usually telling me off about something. While this has certainly improved in my adult years, as a child and teenager there wasn't a lot of emotional connection. When our family discovered the book *The Five Love Languages* by Gary Chapman[2] we realised Dad shows love primarily through acts of service while my number one love language is touch. No wonder we struggled to connect!

But that's not a big deal, right? It's not essential, is it? I survived. I was well-provided for. I got a good education and now I'm a healthy adult and a committed Christian with a great family. Surely nurture and affection is not one of the essential requirements for a dad, but merely an added bonus that we can live without?

I might be able to convince myself that is true if it wasn't for the fact that I grew up desperate for a boyfriend. From as young as I can remember, I desperately wanted someone to hold my hand, to snuggle up to on a Saturday night, to shower me with love and affection, to accept me.

So I can try to convince myself that I don't need the active, affectionate, nurturing love of a father, but the evidence proves the exact opposite. The evidence is the first chapter of this book. As much as I don't like to admit it, I need this kind of love and it never once occurred to me that what I was searching for was the Father's love. It never even crossed my mind. Why not? Because, weirdly enough, I thought I had a good dad.

I thought I knew what a good dad was and it didn't include this affectionate, nurturing kind of love. So I assumed that Father God was exactly the same: God would provide for me, protect me, guide me and (in a distant kind of way) love me. But dote on me? Adore me? Say beautiful things about me? Have an emotional connection with me? No. I knew in my head God loved me and I thought that was enough. When I needed to feel love, it was not my heavenly Father I ran to. I didn't expect that from Him. Why should I?

So when God showed me this kind of love anyway, it staggered me. Like the day my youth leader prayed over me 'God really, really loves you' and I burst into tears, not knowing why. Like the time I did something naughty and then went to youth group and people kept saying, 'God wants someone in this room to know how much He loves you.' I couldn't hold back the tears as the love of God was being poured into my heart in a moment when I knew I didn't deserve it.

THE EMOTIONAL LOVE OF GOD HAS ALWAYS TAKEN ME BY SURPRISE.

I attribute it to Jesus or the Holy Spirit, forgetting that Jesus came to lead us to the Father, and the Holy Spirit pours the love of the Father into our hearts (Romans 5:5). They are all one.

Recently, I have caught snippets of information that referred to research proving the importance of a healthy father-daughter relationship, so I Googled it. I discovered there's way more than a snippet of information! There are decades' worth of research, thousands of studies all pointing to the same thing: a girl really, really needs her daddy's love and affection. A University of Arizona study showed that '90% of teen girls experience "father hunger" when they are not affirmed by their fathers' (Joan Borysenko, PhD).[3] And that 'If a young woman gets that affirmation and approval from her dad, she is not going to be desperate to get it anywhere else because she already has it in him'.[4]

This tells me that a hands-on nurturing father is not just the cultural persuasion of this generation but a God-made need in every female. A girl needs to know – not just intellectually, but emotionally and actually – that her daddy loves her and accepts her and thinks she is amazing, otherwise she will look for that need to be met somewhere else. She will begin the futile, unfulfilled, even promiscuous search for someone or something else to meet that need.

This chapter isn't about hating on our dads or lamenting how rubbish they all are – it is about recognising our needs and saying: it's OK to want more than we have had. We've come full circle to chapter two again! If you are reading this book, chances are you have unmet needs and at least some of those will be because they haven't been met by a father. I know it sounds cheesy, I know it sounds like a cliché, but it might be exactly what you need to know and hear to have a full and satisfying relationship with your heavenly one.

I don't know what kind of father you have – absent, abusive, disapproving, passive or even a good one – but I know he's not perfect. Perhaps your dad is the opposite of mine – great at the hands-on love and affection, but not so great at protection or provision or modelling lifestyle. Whatever your experience, without realising it, your knowledge of your heavenly Father will be flawed until you get to know Him for yourself.

How do I meet the Father?

For me, it has meant taking some deliberate time out in my life to seek Him. Let me backtrack a little.

For the past few years, while my marriage and family life have been wonderful, I have been fighting a losing battle with disappointment. I stopped dreaming altogether because I couldn't handle even one more disappointment. Life became very grey. At the same time, I was desperately searching for some meaning to my life – in the same way that I once desperately searched for a husband.

It was submitting my first draft of this book to a publisher that started the process of meeting my Father – properly. This publishing team includes a counsellor and she was the one who pulled back the blinds to show me that there was a problem. With her help, and that of my husband, my neighbours and a pastoral team at church, I made a decision to stop trying to be the person I think I ought to be and to seek out the Father. (Sound familiar yet?)

I cut back all my commitments to the bare minimum, decluttered my life of 'busyness' and created space for God to reveal Himself to me. I began to wait – deliberately wait on God. (This should really be ringing a few bells by now).

As soon as I made that decision, it was as if some blockage had been removed – a blockage that the Father had been waiting for a really long time to be removed – and every day He began to reveal Himself to me – every day! Every song I listened to, every podcast I played, every Bible reading, every prayer, suddenly became meaningful and had a personal message in it directly to me. I cried a lot. And for the first time in almost three years, I began to hear God's voice clearly again.

At the same time, I battled with every fear I've ever felt. Every negative thought that had ever fluttered past suddenly came home to roost. I created space in my day after every counselling session in order to process my thoughts, and each time, God would reveal another bit of Himself.

One example was listening to a podcast from Gateway Church in Texas, USA – it was a guest speaker and when he talked about Jesus on the cross being separated from His Father when the sky went black, I had a revelation. I suddenly realised that Jesus knows exactly how I feel – He knows how it feels to have moments of complete darkness when all hope seems lost and you just have to keep going even when you feel completely alone. Jesus knew how I felt and I took so much comfort from that because it meant I hadn't failed, it was just a valley I was walking through. Jesus had walked through it already and come out the other side, triumphant. Now He was walking with me through that same well-trodden valley so I would come out the other side too. A light began to shine at the end of the tunnel. As the song 'Good, Good Father' came on after the podcast, I was so aware of the presence of God in the room, comforting me.

On my lowest day, the day when I felt at my absolute worst, with every negative thought I'd ever felt pounding inside my head, I had an email from an old friend, full of words of encouragement. They were more than that – her words were the exact opposite of every fear and doubt I'd been battling. It was that specific. In my darkest moment of need, God prompted an old friend from the other side of the world to write the exact words I needed to hear. Dare I believe it? Is that how much God loves me? Did God really do that just for me? Yes, I believe He did.

I went to Hillsong's Colour Conference in London and the theme was 'Be Found'. It was written in big letters everywhere you looked. That was God's message to me that week – that God sees me and knows and has chosen me. We sang the song 'Love on the Line' and I sang at the top of my voice, proclaiming the words by faith because I wasn't *feeling* the truth of the lyrics at that time. Even last week, when I faced another disappointment, the same song came on in the background! God's message to me is to remember that it is in Him I am found, and in His love and grace I can stand and not be overcome.

I think, while writing this book, God has taken me through the exact same process of looking for love all over again because the process wasn't yet complete. I had been married eleven years, but I was searching again. I was desperate for a role in life that gave me meaning, just like I was desperate for a boyfriend as a girl. Both times, I had deep needs crying out to be met, and I was trying to fill them with 'stuff' rather than look to God.

It took someone else to help me see that I had a need, just like Jamie helped me see my need, as I mentioned earlier. What did I actually do that made the difference between the horny girl and the satisfied woman? Not much, God did most of it. I think all I really did was allow God to move and work in my life. I created a few boundaries to keep away distractions, and gave God space. And I waited. Both times, I've waited on God. And just like last time, it's been really, really hard to wait.

There have been plenty of opportunities to jump ahead and try to make something happen myself – I had several job offers that would have been lucrative, but would have meant giving up on my calling to be a missionary in the modern world. Social action projects caught my eye, as well as studying theology and an offer to go on a preaching rota that would have played havoc with our family life, my husband's job and our church commitments. I was distracted with the need to start a business for a while, but all of these were 'Wrong One' or even 'Almost Right One' options. I said no to all of them – even the tempting ones – and waited. It was time to stop wasting my life pursuing wrong, or even 'good' options, and to wait on God. In the meantime, I was not idle (I wrote this book, for one thing!) and God continued to teach me about self-discipline, perseverance, how to deal with disappointments, and so many other things.

I believe now that God knew this book wasn't finished – it was missing the Father.

An encounter with my heavenly Father

When I first asked the pastoral team at church to pray for me, they didn't do much praying but a lot of talking, and then asked me to pray. They said to me: 'What do you want to say to your Father?' And do you know? I couldn't think of a single thing. I had absolutely nothing to say to Him. Conversations with my own dad have always been a bit stilted (sorry, Dad), so why would I have anything to say to a heavenly one?

Then in my mind, I saw Jesus kneeling and looking over to the left. Usually when I pray, I see Jesus dancing. Probably because we both love to dance. But this time Jesus was kneeling. *Where's the Holy Spirit?* I wondered. He was right next to me, also kneeling and also looking left. Both Jesus and the Holy Spirit, members of the Trinity I was most familiar with, were waiting expectantly for something and they were so excited for me. It occurred to me then that the Father must be coming. I wasn't sure how I felt about that, to be honest. A bit nervous, maybe?

But there wasn't time to think too much because then, over to the left, there was a bright light coming closer to me. It was bright white, but softer yellow around the edges. It was lovely. It was warm and lovely and it was soft. I don't mean soft as in sissy-soft, but when I think about people who are soft on the inside – it was that kind of soft. A kindness, a loveliness was emanating from Him. There was no hard exterior, there was just the lovely, soft kindness for all to see. The feeling only lasted a moment and then it was time to go.

As I shared this with my counsellor the next day, I realised I had always assumed God had a hard exterior. While I know God is love, I made an assumption, based on my experience of my earthly dad, that all that loveliness was on the inside and there was a hard exterior preventing me from feeling it. In all probability, I too had a hard exterior when it came to being honest and open with the Father. How could I have it so wrong? He's lovely! He's wonderful!

As I was preparing to write this chapter, I was reminded of the popular 'I Can Only Imagine' song sung by MercyMe[5] that wonders how we might respond when we finally get to meet the Father in heaven. Until now, I've always thought I would dance for Him – I'd show Him what I can do so He can be proud of me.

I have always wanted to impress God and make Him notice me. I've lived as if life is some big audition. Guilt over past mistakes had left me with the same servant attitude as the prodigal son when he made the decision to return home: willing to serve the father but not feeling worthy to join him at the family table. But slowly, step by step, my heavenly Father has drawn me home. He already knows what I can do, He already sees me dance nearly every time I worship. I don't have to prove a single thing to Him. He already loves me enough to send His Son, Jesus, to die for me, and Jesus has taken my sin and replaced it with His righteousness. I'm no longer just a servant, I'm called a friend of God, I have been given the right to be called a child of God and I am being prepared to be the bride of Christ. When that moment of being face-to-face finally comes, how will I resist running up and into all that soft, warm, powerful, enveloping loveliness?

Think about the children who ran up to Jesus in Luke 18:15–17. They just wanted Jesus to touch them and to bless them, maybe a hug or a ruffle of the hair, or maybe even a playful wrestle. But the disciples were so used to God being the kind of God who was separated from us by the curtain in Jerusalem's temple[6] that this kind of love and enthusiasm seemed out of place. So what was it Jesus said? He said that this is what the kingdom of God is all about. And then He went even further and said everyone who wants into God's kingdom needs to receive it like a child.

How does a child receive something? Do they study it intellectually? Do they read about it or hear about it and mull it over? Or do they reach for it and grab it and want to experience it for themselves?

When my husband came home the other day with a bunch of flowers for me and a single pink geranium for each of the children, my reaction was to look at them and say, 'That's nice, can you put them in water, please? I'm busy making dinner.' My girls' reaction was completely different! First they ran to the door when Daddy was home, both wanting to be the one to let him in. Then they squealed with delight at both the gift and the giver. They gave not one thought to water and vases until they had their fill of hugs and kisses with the gift-giver himself, their daddy.

THE FATHER IS NOT THERE TO BE STUDIED OR JUST LEARNED ABOUT. HE IS OUR FATHER, TO KNOW AND BE KNOWN BY!

He wants to bless us and to love us and to meet every single one of those five needs in us.[7] All our needs – physical, spiritual, intellectual and emotional. That's what He's like.

When I think back to the young woman who looked in the mirror and said, 'You're not all I need, Lord. I also need a man', I had no idea who I was talking to! I really did not know the Father at all. I still needed a man for some things – like in order to have children, for one thing – but it was God, the source of all love, the giver of all good gifts, who gave me that man! However, that man was never given so he could meet all my needs. I still need the love of a Father. Not just as a one-off experience, but every single day. My husband is wonderful, and he meets as many of my needs as he possibly can. But he's not God. And if I ask him to be, I'll suck him dry. This year has shown me that I really, really, really need my heavenly Father, every single day.

What's your story? And where do you want it to go from here?

Get real with God

Which type (or types) of father have you personally experienced?

Good Absent Abusive Disapproving Passive

Let's take a look at those five needs a father meets, and ask yourself which of these were met by your own father/father figure and to what extent. A 5 indicates that role was fully satisfied in your life, a 0 is the opposite.

Protection	0	1	2	3	4	5
Provision	0	1	2	3	4	5
Nurture/Affection	0	1	2	3	4	5
Training/Modelling Lifestyle	0	1	2	3	4	5
Personal Guidance	0	1	2	3	4	5

Do you notice any similarities or parallels with your answers from chapter two? Go back and have a look, then write them here:

Is it easy or difficult for you to believe that God is the perfect Father?

Why?

May I encourage you to spend a little time with God in the next twenty-four hours, and ask Him to reveal Himself to you as a Father? You might want to ask your mentor or youth leader or someone from the pastoral team at your church to do this with you. If it is the right time to explore this, you may want to meet a few times in a safe place. For now, would you pray this prayer with me?

Dear God,
I believe that Jesus died for me so that I could, without hesitation, call You 'my Father' and for that to be a real, present, everyday relationship. Please would You reveal Yourself to me as my Father? Show me if I have any wrong understanding about what that means. Please show me what it means to have a real, present, everyday Father-daughter relationship with You. Thank You, Lord Jesus, that You made the way, that You showed us the way, and that You are the way to the Father.
Amen.

Chapter Fifteen
A Vision of the End Goal

I liken you, my darling, to a mare
among Pharaoh's chariot horses.
(Song of Solomon 1:9, NIV UK 2011)

'Many years ago, a beloved friend made the journey from Suez to Cairo in the cumbrous diligence then in use [translation: horse-driven coaches]. On arrival in Suez, the passengers took their places. About a dozen wild young horses were harnessed with ropes to the vehicle, the driver took his seat and cracked his whip, and the horses dashed off, some to the right, some to the left and others forward, causing the coach to start with a bound, and as suddenly stop, with the effect of first throwing those sitting in the front seat into the laps of those sitting behind, and then of reversing the operation. With the help of sufficient Arabs running on each side to keep these wild animals progressing in the right direction the passengers were jerked and jolted, bruised and shaken, until on reaching their destination, they were too wearied and sore to take the rest they so much needed.'

That was a real-life story. I adapted it slightly from Hudson Taylor's commentary on the Song of Solomon.[1] Can you imagine being there? Can you imagine being one of the unfortunate passengers landing on the lap of a stranger because of unruly horses?

Now imagine the opposite situation. Imagine you are the passenger and those horses are highly skilled, well-trained Arabian horses, the breed that once carried kings into battle and paraded pharaohs through the capital cities of the ancient world. They are the horse equivalent of a Ferrari. These horses love and trust their masters so completely that they need only be called and they instantly trot over. Then they stand perfectly still while you all mount. You feel so at ease. There's no jostling or jerking. In their care, your journey is restful and quick. You can admire the scenery and get to know the other passengers. It is also peaceful. These horses don't need to be shouted at and rarely need the reminder of a whip – they're sensitive to the slightest nudges and gentlest whispers of their master.

Meekness

What is the difference between the two kinds of horses? Both types are strong and have the potential to be amazing and accomplish incredible things. But only one of them fulfils that potential. The difference between them can be described with one word: meekness. Not a word we use much today and even when we do use it we don't really understand it. Even though Dictionary.com[2] says 'overly submissive or compliant; spiritless; tame' as only the *second* definition of 'meekness', it is usually the one we think of first. But that's not what Jesus was talking about when he said 'The meek will inherit earth'.[3] Not at all!

Meekness is the opposite of rebellion and independence – two words valued more highly by Westerners than by Jesus.

MEEKNESS IS STRENGTH UNDER SUBMISSION –

– strength given to someone greater, for something greater than simply our own short-lived pleasure. One of the flattering descriptions of the bride in the Song of Solomon is that she is like a female horse in Pharaoh's hand-picked, best-of-the-best company (1:9).

You see, a meek horse is not one who has lost her strength, but one who has offered her strength to the service of her master.

Can you picture the company of finely apparelled horses, muscles rippling and flexing under their ornaments, standing in perfect unison, utterly still till they feel the slightest twitch of their master's thigh telling them to move in one accord? A meek horse doesn't need to be whipped or beaten into submission, she only needs a gentle pull or prod or whisper from her master, whose voice is so familiar to her. And a meek horse will not run away when it sees the enemy coming, but will trust her master and hold her ground. A meek horse will be the one who wins the battle because she does not rely on her own strength. A meek horse will walk a smoother path because she is guided by one who knows the way. And the meek horse gets the greatest privilege a horse can get, the greatest reward imaginable. She gets to carry the king. When we, the bride, are compared to a filly of Pharaoh's class, it reminds us that there is a reward to meekness, to submitting our strength to Him: we get to carry the King. We get to glorify and lift up and carry the presence of King Jesus wherever we go.

Your vision

What kind of a Christian do you want to be? Do you prefer to run free like a wild horse, enjoying every blessing life has to offer, but only for your own enjoyment, regardless of the consequences to others? Wild horses look attractive from a distance, but try to get close to one and you'll find they're dangerous and ultimately useless. All the incredible things that could be accomplished by that power and strength come to nothing when that strength is only used for personal pleasure. In Proverbs 29:11 'casting off restraint' is synonymous with 'perishing' or dying (Compare NIV with NKJV). This means that casting off restraint, while it may sound wonderful, ultimately leads to death because we have no self-control. When we have no self-control, circumstances quickly gain control over us. Like Elsa in Disney's *Frozen*, 'Let It Go' may make for a number one single but it also left her isolated and alone, only able to hurt the people she loved the most. But for those of us who don't struggle to keep control of our magical abilities to create ice, here are some other real-life examples: if we can't control our mouths, sooner or later we will hurt others with our words and find ourselves alone. If we can't control our consumption of alcohol, sooner or later the addiction to alcohol will control us and cause us to hurt others, especially those we love the most. It is the same with our love lives.

IF WE CAST OFF ALL RESTRAINT AND LIVE ONLY FOR THE LUST OF THE MOMENT, OUR INTIMACY WITH GOD WILL SLOWLY BEGIN TO SUFFER...

...and we will wonder where He has gone.

Is the answer marriage? Well, marriage is the answer to a lot of questions. But is it the answer to yours? Is it the one thing you need in order to satisfy your soul? Marriage satisfies a lot of things, but it is a finite source for your bottomless cup of love.

I was once told by a youth leader that I ought to get married, and quick (he saw the desperation oozing out of me and figured that marriage would solve my problem). I was so happy to go back to that person and tell him that I hadn't got married yet, but I had found something far better and that was Jesus. Jesus was the man of my dreams and God was my Source, the person I now turned to whenever I was in need.

For those of us looking for love, it is not enough to just be a Christian and assume the first man you end up with is God's choice for you. If we want God to pick someone out for us, we need to first offer our hearts and our love lives to Him. And then we need to let Him be God and do what He does best, not taking back control at the first sign of temptation.

The reason the Lord asks us to offer ourselves to Him is so that we can fulfil the potential He has put in us – so He can harness our strength, train and develop it and direct it in such a way that we bring Him glory, help others, contribute to the kingdom of God in that unique way that He designed for each of us, and carry the presence of King Jesus wherever we go. It doesn't mean you never get to run free – it means when the times come to run free, you do so in a way that brings only joy to you and others around you. It means having the courage to go for it and being free to accept God's good gifts when they are given.

Wouldn't you love to spend your life knowing that you are doing exactly what you have been made to do and absolutely loving it? This is the fulfilment of Ephesians 2:10: 'For we are His workmanship, created in Christ Jesus for good works, which God prepared beforehand that we should walk in them.'

But what if...?

Sometimes we are afraid that God will not fulfil His promises. What will God do with my heart once He has it? Will He forget all about it? Will He treat it badly? No, we know He won't do that, but what if He chooses an ugly person to teach me to value inner beauty? What if I offer my love life to Jesus and He doesn't give me a husband? What if I let Him choose my husband and He chooses someone I wouldn't choose? Or makes me wait for more years than I can handle? What if... what if... what if...

Equally scarily, what if we submit our love lives to God and He gives us a husband? I know this sounds crazy, but a 'No' from God, while painful, leads us directly into His arms of love, which is a familiar, safe place to be. A 'Yes' from God is like being released to fly, and flying is scary too! What about those safe arms under me? Are they going to disappear? What is it like out there in the sky? Will I be able to handle it? What if I fall? Will the arms still be there to catch me? What if I am wrong or make a mistake or risk everything and lose?

These...

...'WHAT IF'S' ARE THE STRUGGLE WE GO THROUGH BEFORE WE SUBMIT OUR STRENGTH TO JESUS –

– before we offer the Father our pearls – and the only way to overcome them is to trust the Father, that He is good and He loves you, and His plans for you are for good and not for evil, 'to give you a future and a hope'.[4] He wants a bride, remember? Not a slave. He's not trying to break you; He is trying to win your heart. There is not one promise He has ever broken, not one prophecy that will not be fulfilled.

He is offering you the chance to let Him lead you and share life with you. 'My yoke is easy and My burden is light' Jesus said (Matthew 11:30). In the days when Jesus said that, everyone knew that a yoke was a plank of wood that strapped two oxen side by side so they could work in the field together and share the load. While oxen of equal strength are preferable, if one of the pair was stronger than the other, the bulk of the load would be transferred onto the stronger one and the weaker one would walk slightly in front, so that they didn't have the demoralising role of always having to catch up.[5] When Jesus offers us to take up His yoke, He offers us a partnership in which He is the stronger one. He carries the bulk of the load. With the Father at the reins and the Holy Spirit strengthening you, you have found what you were looking for. You are headed for the goal.

The end goal

This is the end goal: to run to the Father, with Jesus, in good times and in bad. For your relationship with God to be ever-growing, ever-deepening and always first. To enjoy the highs when they come and persevere together through the lows, allowing Him to carry you, lead you and guide you. To trust that the valleys will not last forever, that you will grow through them and that there is a great view from the top of the next mountain.

And what about in a marriage? What does a relationship with Jesus at the centre look like? Maybe a bit like this:

To be excited with Jesus as you take the first steps into a new relationship with a seemingly flawless man who loves you; to run back to Him if that man hurts you or disappoints you; to thank God every time that man brings you joy; to thank God every time that man sees through your outer façade and reveals the ugly truths of your not-yet perfect character; to allow God to love you when you mess up and disappoint your man, and to allow God to teach you to love him better even when it's hard. To hold on to God while you persevere through life's challenges and trials and tests. To ask God to fill your heart full of love for your man when you feel like you have run out. To thank God in those moments of boundless joy when you and your man experience something wonderful or reach new heights in your relationship, and to allow God to draw you closer together when facing situations that would throw most couples apart. To forgive and be forgiven by the power of Jesus. To love and be loved with the boundless love of the Father.

That through every high and through every low, you do not demand that your needs be met by the other, but you instead recognise God, your Father, is the Source of everlasting love, and trust Jesus as the centre of your relationship, the third strand in your cord that strengthens you and binds you with love.[6] Your joy is found in trusting that your Father will provide for all your needs and your desires so that you can fully enjoy everything your man has to offer with a thankful, not a needy or critical heart.

JESUS IS NOT THE CONSOLATION PRIZE FOR THE UNMARRIED OR LONELY – HE IS THE ONE AND ONLY PRIZE!

He is the end goal. Whether you are single or married, you can stop looking for love – you have found Him. He has always been there and He always will be.

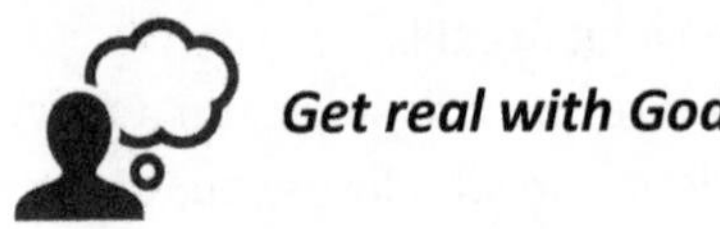

Get real with God

What has stood out to you most in this chapter?

What is a meek horse capable of doing that a wild horse isn't? Can you apply this to your life?

What are your 'What if...' questions?

Where will your relationship with Jesus go from here? Where do you want it to go?

Epilogue: Love Lost and Love Found Again

In the beginning God created the heavens and the earth ...
Then God said, 'Let Us make man in Our image, according to Our likeness ...'
(Genesis 1:1,26)

There exists a Trinity called Love. Glorious, majestic, beautiful and awesome; their surpassing greatness is equal only to their holiness, and their immense love for one another is as pure as it is intense. So perfect, so intimate is this love and so perfect is their unity of thought, word and deed that though they are three, they are one. They are Trinity, yet they think, feel and decide as one being, one entity, one God. They are holy and they are whole.

THEY ARE PERFECT AND COMPLETE IN ONE ANOTHER'S PRESENCE; A THREE-STRANDED CORD BOUND TOGETHER IN LOVE.

Trinity are the uncreated Creator. Their love is generous. Their joy, proceeding from their undefiled relationship, constantly bubbles over and it is their pleasure to create beings to receive the overflow of their love.

One day, they agreed to make a people – a masterpiece – that would reflect their own image and likeness. They would carry characteristics from each member of the Trinity in their design. This masterpiece would hold the capacity for love – the ability and the vulnerability to receive the love of the Creator and to share it with each other.

Once they had decided, they did it. They created a people of both male and female and they called them Adam. The race of Adam was like the Trinity in so many ways, but it was not made of the same substance as the Trinity. It was a created people, made only of dust and, while they reflected the glory of their Creator, they were yet reliant on their Creator as their source of purpose and love. This is why there were only two – a male and a female. The Creator Himself was the third strand required for completion, for unity, for an unbroken cord of love.

In order to give the male and female the joy of discovering one another, the Creator formed the male first. When the male looked and realised his need, his lack, his desire for another, the Creator discreetly formed the female and then revealed her to him for the first time.

Oh, the rapture of that first unveiling! If ever there was a love at first sight it was then, in the Garden of Eden, at the beginning of all creation. The male's joy at finding the one he'd been looking for and her exquisite delight in being found and enjoyed was resounding music in an echoing chasm, laughter on a barren plain and a spring of water to a thirsty soul.

The Trinity looked and saw that it was very, very good.

Every day, Adam would walk together with their Creator in the Garden of Eden – the garden of pleasure – in the cool of the day. It was the highlight of their day, the part Adam most looked forward to. When they walked together with their Creator God they knew love in all its fullness and it brought unbroken peace, contentment, joy and satisfaction. He was their everlasting Source and nothing at all came between them in those beautiful, wonder-filled days.

But then Adam was broken.

What the future of Adam might have been had they trusted the word of their Creator we can never know. It was lost on that dark day. It was the day they listened to the deceiver and allowed the sin of pride and rebellion to enter their hearts and turn their heads away from their God. The three-stranded cord unravelled. They became Adam and Eve and instead of walking with each other and with their God they walked one behind the other, hidden and separate from their God. Neither of them would ever again know the unbroken intimacy of Eden. They instead had to be satisfied with what leftovers they could carry with them, in their hearts, as they were hurriedly and swiftly removed from the garden wherein grew the Tree of Life. Should they eat from it, they would live forever in their sin and all hope for humankind would be lost.

Joy now came only temporarily, in fleeting moments that melted in their hands as they tried to hold on to it. And it brought pain. Too often it was marred with selfishness, lust and a garish pile of other sins. They no longer knew love in the unbroken way they had been designed to, but the need for completeness was still in their hearts.

Few of those born after Eden experienced the pure love of the Creator filling their hearts to overflowing. But all of them knew lack. Need. An unfulfilled desire. And the desperation to fill it with something – anything – that might promise fulfilment. Adam and Eve's son, Cain, filled his heart with revenge; others grasped at power. Later came possessions and gold, false gods and idols, money and gluttonous desires.

The joy they once had in discovering each other now became a desperate hunt for satisfaction and while they still needed each other, loved each other and brought joy to each other's lives, it was no longer given and received from a place of completeness but from a desperate, thirsty desire for more. No matter how hard they tried, how many things they tried, no matter how many ways they tried, their expressions of love for each other were like moonbeams to a flower that craves only the sun. They promised so much more than they were able to deliver.

As one generation passed to another, there were some who held onto the seed of hope that the Creator had promised to Adam in their final moments in Eden. The hope that one day, a man would be born who would be the one. He would restore what was broken, reform the three-stranded cord and bridge the gap between the race of Adam and their Creator God, so once more they could enjoy unbroken communion. He would be the last of the race of Adam and the first of a new race of Man – a race that through Him could have access to the Source of everlasting love and enjoy union once more with their Creator. The Creator whose love alone was deep and wide and pure enough to bring completeness, joy and satisfaction.

THE CREATOR ALONE COULD MEET THE NEED THAT HAD DELIBERATELY BEEN PUT IN THEIR HEARTS FROM THE VERY BEGINNING, AND IT WAS THE CREATOR'S PLEASURE TO DO SO.

Many, many years later, when the time was right, there was a woman. Walking towards the well in the heat of the day, when no one else was around, heart reaching out to heaven, she believed for an answer, not knowing how or when that answer would come.[1] Perhaps it was her glimmer of faith that shone against the backdrop of a dark and cynical world that caught the attention of the one.

A man spoke to her. A man who had not just seen her but saw the heart within her that shone, just as He had seen Nathanael, sitting under the fig tree. It was Jesus.

'A time is coming', Jesus said to her, 'and has now come when the true worshippers will worship the Father in Spirit and in truth, for they are the kind of worshippers the Father seeks.'[2]

All this time she had been looking for love and every one of her five husbands had let her down. Even the good ones, the ones from good families with kind hands who had so raised her expectations – even they had failed to fill her ever-thirsty soul for more love, more affection, more attention, more passion. One by one she had searched and searched. No one had ever told her that perhaps she was not the only one searching. No one had ever suggested that the true Source of love, God Himself, might be searching, sweeping the earth with his eyes, looking for her. As a father looks for his prodigal son, as a woman looks for her lost coin, as a shepherd looks for his sheep, He was looking for her. Could it be true?

Yet here was this man, this prophet, who sat before her and made her a promise – He promised that His 'living water' would quench her thirsty soul forever. What a hope! What a promise! Could it possibly be true? Was He really talking about water? Was He really talking about her? All she knew was that she was lost and the Perfect Man, the one who had been promised from the very beginning, had forsaken heaven's glory and splendour and now walked the earth in search of hidden treasure, just like her. At last, at last, she could stop searching. At last, at last, she had been found.

Recommended Further Reading

Father's Love

Jack Frost, *Spiritual Slavery to Spiritual Sonship* (Shippensburg, PA: Destiny Image, 2013).
Floyd McClung, *The Father Heart of God* (Eastbourne: Kingsway, 2001).
Ed Piorek, *The Father Loves You: An Invitation to Perfect Love* (South Africa: Vineyard International Publishing, 1999).
Sy Rogers, *Keeping Clean* (Trilogy CD) www.syrogers.com (accessed 20.12.16).
Sy Rogers, *Smart Relating* (Trilogy CD) www.syrogers.com (accessed 20.12.16).

The Bride of Christ

Stephanie Cottam, *Ready or Not – He is Coming* (Saffron Walden: Glory to Glory Publications, 2013).
Shannon Ethridge, *Completely His: Loving Jesus Without Limits* (Colorado Springs, CO: WaterBrook, 2008).
Francine Rivers, *Redeeming Love* (Colorado Springs, CO: Multnomah Publishers, 1997).
Hudson Taylor, *Union and Communion* (Originally published in 1983, it has been re-printed by several publishers. I like the version by Alpha International [London: 2004].)

Marriage

Timothy Keller, *The Meaning of Marriage* (USA: Hodder & Stoughton, 2013).

Hearing God's Voice

Loren Cunningham, *Is that Really You, God?* (Edmonds, WA: YWAM Publishing, 1984).
Joy Dawson, *Forever Ruined for the Ordinary* (YWAM Publishing: USA, 1998).
Priscilla Shirer, *Discerning the Voice of God* (Chicago, IL: Moody Publishers, 2006).

End Notes

Chapter Two

1. Twelve steps programme. See: Bill Wilson (2001). *Alcoholics Anonymous: The Original 1939 Edition* (Dover Publications: USA)
2. For example, *Hierarchy of Needs: A Theory of Human Motivation* by Abraham H. Maslow was a model developed between 1943–54 and is still studied, built upon and used extensively today.
3. Human Givens Institute: http://www.hgi.org.uk/archive/human-givens.htm#.Vdt-Vf-FN7h (accessed 7.12.16).
4. David Ferguson, Don McMinn, *Top 10 Intimacy Needs* (Austin, TX: Intimacy Press, 1994).

Chapter Three

1. 2 Corinthians 4:17–18: 'For our light affliction, which is but for a moment, is working for us a far more exceeding and eternal weight of glory, while we do not look at the things which are seen, but at the things which are not seen. For the things which are seen are temporary, but the things which are not seen are eternal.'
2. Matthew 6:19–20: 'Do not lay up for yourselves treasures on earth, where moth and rust destroy and where thieves break in and steal; but lay up for yourselves treasures in heaven, where neither moth nor rust destroys and where thieves do not break in and steal.'
3. Philippians 4:8: 'Finally, brethren, whatever things are true, whatever things are noble, whatever things are just, whatever things are pure, whatever things are lovely, whatever things are of good report, if there is any virtue and if there is anything praiseworthy – meditate on these things.'
4. NIV UK 2011.
5. *Love Story* (1970)
6. Hebrews 10:25: 'not forsaking the assembling of ourselves together, as is the manner of some, but exhorting one another, and so much the more as you see the Day approaching'.

Chapter Four

1. 'The Form of Solemnization of Marriage' from *The Book of Common Prayer.*

2. The kingdom of God was never mentioned in the Old Testament. The idea of the Church, God dwelling in the hearts of people, the kingdom of God that is not of this world was referred to by Paul as a great mystery that was hidden but has been revealed through Christ. Ephesians 3:1–12; Colossians 1:25–27; Romans 11:25.

3. Derek Prince, *Rediscovering God's Church* (Baldock: Derek Prince Ministries UK, 2006).

4. Mark 1:23–25: 'Now there was a man in their synagogue with an unclean spirit. And he cried out, saying, "Let us alone! What have we to do with You, Jesus of Nazareth? Did You come to destroy us? I know who You are – the Holy One of God!" But Jesus rebuked him, saying, "Be quiet, and come out of him!"'

5. John 6:15: 'Therefore when Jesus perceived that they were about to come and take Him by force to make Him king, He departed again to the mountain by Himself alone.'

6. John 2:24–25: 'But Jesus would not entrust himself to them, for he knew all people. He did not need any testimony about mankind, for he knew what was in each person.' (NIV UK 2011)

7. Matthew 16:14: 'They replied, "Some say John the Baptist; others say Elijah; and still others, Jeremiah or one of the prophets.' (NIV UK 2011)

8. Mark 10:17–18: 'As Jesus started on his way, a man ran up to him and fell on his knees before him. "Good teacher," he asked, "what must I do to inherit eternal life?" "Why do you call me good?" Jesus answered. "No one is good – except God alone.' (NIV UK 2011)

9. Matthew 3:16–18: 'When He had been baptized, Jesus came up immediately from the water; and behold, the heavens were opened to Him, and He saw the Spirit of God descending like a dove and alighting upon Him. And suddenly a voice came from heaven, saying, "This is My beloved Son, in whom I am well pleased."'

10. Matthew 17:5: 'While he was still speaking, behold, a bright cloud overshadowed them; and suddenly a voice came out of the cloud, saying, "This is My beloved Son, in whom I am well pleased. Hear Him!"'

11. Joyce Meyer, *Help Me I'm Married!* (NY: Warner Books, 2001)

12. Romans 8:28: 'And we know that all things work together for good to those who love God, to those who are the called according to His purpose.'

Jeremiah 29:11: 'For I know the thoughts that I think toward you, says the LORD, thoughts of peace and not of evil, to give you a future and a hope.'

13. Hebrews 13:8: 'Jesus Christ is the same yesterday, today, and forever.'

Malachi 3:6: 'For I am the LORD, I do not change ...'

Chapter Five

1. http://northpoint.org/messages/staying-in-love (accessed 7.12.16).

2. Tim and Beverly LaHaye, *The Act of Marriage* (Grand Rapids, MI: Zondervan, 1998)

3. Jesus said: 'But those things which proceed out of the mouth come from the heart, and they defile a man. For out of the heart proceed evil thoughts, murders, adulteries, fornications, thefts, false witness, blasphemies. These are the things which defile a man ...' (Matthew 15:18–20).

4. According to an article by Drs John Diggs and Eric Keroack, 'People who have misused their sexual faculty and become bonded to multiple persons will diminish the power of oxytocin to maintain a permanent bond with an individual.' http://lifesubjects.blogspot.co.uk/2009/01/premarital-sex.html (accessed 7.12.16).

5. http://www.markgungorshow.com/wordpress/wp-content/uploads/Delaying-Sex-Shown-to-Be-Key-to-a-Happy-Marriage.pdf (accessed 7.12.16)

6. http://socialpathology.blogspot.co.uk/2012/03/promiscuity-data-

guest-post.html (accessed 7.12.16).

7. Fornication in Webster's 1828 Dictionary:

1. The incontinence or lewdness of unmarried persons, male or female; also, the criminal conversation of a married man with an unmarried woman.

2. Adultery. Matthew 5:32.

3. Incest. 1 Corinthians 5:1.

4. Idolatry; a forsaking of the true God, and worshipping of idols. 2 Chronicles 21:11, Revelation 19:2.

8. Debauchery means 'Chiefly, habitual lewdness; excessive unlawful indulgence of lust', Websters Dictionary 1828.

9. Lasciviousness as defined in Webster's 1828 Dictionary:

'1. Looseness; irregular indulgence of animal desires; wantonness; lustfulness. Who, being past feeling, have given themselves over to lasciviousness. Eph 4[:19].

2. Tendency to excite lust, and promote irregular indulgences.'

10. Mark 7:22, 2 Corinthians 12:21, Galatians 5:19, Ephesians 4:19, 1 Peter 4:3,

11. Psalm 66:10–12:

'God, you have tested us.
You put us through fire to make us like silver.
You put us in prison.
You placed heavy loads on our backs.
You let our enemies ride their chariots over our heads.
We went through fire and water.
But you brought us to a place
where we have everything we need.' (NIRV)

Chapter Six

1. J. Strong et al, *The Strongest Strong's exhaustive concordance of the Bible 21st Century Ed.* (Grand Rapids, MI: Zondervan, 2001): 'this [word] can range in meaning from the mere acquisition and understanding of information to intimacy in relationship, including

sexual relations.'

2. Romans 5:3–4: 'We also glory in tribulations, knowing that tribulation produces perseverance; and perseverance, character; and character, hope.' James 1:2–4: 'Count it all joy when you fall into various trials, knowing that the testing of your faith produces patience. But let patience have its perfect work, that you may be perfect and complete, lacking nothing.'

3. As he sat in church, he was suddenly convicted of his own sin in a profound way. He tried to live better afterwards but he couldn't do it – he was trying to 'be good' rather than allow Jesus into his life. It didn't last, of course.

4. On another occasion Jesus said: 'In the world you will have tribulation; but be of good cheer, I have overcome the world' (John 16:33).

5. Hebrews 12:2, NASB

Chapter Seven

1. The idea of 'Positive Psychology' is a branch of psychology that focuses on building strengths (instead of only addressing the negative) through positive approaches and thought processes. Maslow started it in 1954 (book entitled *Motivation and Personality* [NY: Harper]) and others have written about it since, e.g.:

- Martin E.P. Seligman; Mihaly Csikszentmihalyi (2000). 'Positive Psychology: An Introduction', American Psychologist 55 (1): 5–14.
- Christopher Peterson (2009). 'Positive psychology', Reclaiming Children and Youth 18 (2): 3–7

2. It is traditionally thought that Psalms 120–134, the Songs of Ascents, were sung by the Jews as they climbed the path leading up to Jerusalem for religious festivals, e.g. the feast of unleavened bread, the feast of weeks, or the feast of tabernacles. (See The Lion Handbook to the Bible 4th edition [Oxford: Lion, 2009], p. 387.) As they walked, they would naturally have to look up to see the temple where God rested His feet.

3. 'The Heavenly Vision' by Helen Howarth Lemmel, published in the United Methodist Hymnal 1922.
4. This was a reference to a story I had heard about a man being shown around God's house in heaven and there was one room that made God very sad and God didn't want to show it to the man but the man insisted. When the door was opened it was crammed full and piled high with presents. The man was amazed and said, 'Why are you keeping this door shut? This room is amazing!' And God replied that these were the gifts that His children didn't want. The story demonstrates that God has gifts for us because He loves us but we reject them in order to try to earn them ourselves, a bit like the older brother in the prodigal son story. Grace is a gift, but how many people have rejected it? The Bible says we have been given every spiritual blessing in the heavenly places in Christ (Ephesians 1:3) – yet how many of us needlessly live in spiritual hunger and poverty because we do not understand how loved we are and how good God is?
5. Deuternomy 33:27.
6. Psalm 91.
7. Deuteronomy 31:6,8.

Chapter Eight
1. There are several tests that act like sieves, through which a prophetic word should be sifted to see if it is legitimate: agreement with the word of God (Acts 17:11, Revelation 19:10 says: 'The Spirit of prophecy tells the truth about Jesus.' [NIRV]), peace in your inner Spirit (Romans 8:16), and confirmation from other prayerful disciples of Jesus (1 Corinthians 14:29 says: "Let two or three prophets speak, and let the others judge.")
2. Sex before marriage is called fornication, which is described as 'desires of our own corrupted souls, not the desire of the Spirit of God living in us'. See Matthew 15:19; Mark 7:21; 2 Corinthians 12:21; Galatians 5:19; Ephesians 5:3; Colossians 3:5.
Sex outside of marriage is adultery. 'Do not commit adultery' is the

seventh commandment (Exodus 20:14, NIRV) and Jesus reinforced this boundary and then went even further, saying lustful thoughts (thinking about someone in a sexual way who is not your wife) is adultery of the heart.

3. Leviticus 18:6–18.

4. An example of a community matter might be that you decide to work with an organisation and they ask that you don't date for your first year. Or you work overseas as a missionary and your first priority is to serve them, not shop for a spouse. Another example might be if your parents have put boundaries in place, and if you're still living with them you should definitely respect those.

5. Dr Seuss, *Oh, The Places You'll Go!* (London: HarperCollins, 1990).

6. 'Therefore, assuming a lunar calendar of 360 days, Noah was on the ark for approximately 370 days.' http://www.gotquestions.org/Noahs-ark-questions.html#ixzz3SOlz6wAm (accessed 7.12.16).

Chapter Nine

1. Jehovah-Jireh, one of the many names of God, meaning God is my provider (see Genesis 22:14).

Chapter Ten

1. He drove for seven hours to pick Joanna and me up from Gatwick Airport, in order to drive us the relatively miniscule one hour journey home. Must have been love.

Chapter Eleven

1.https://fastpray.wordpress.com/2014/05/25/coffee-with-perry-noble/ (accessed 7.12.16).

Chapter Twelve

1. Lisa and Andy are pseudonyms to protect the anonymity of my interviewees.

2. Jonah 2:8, NIV 1984.

3. Philip Yancey, *What's So Amazing About Grace?* (Grand Rapids, MI: Zondervan, 2002).

Chapter Thirteen

1. Remember after breakfast on the beach, when Peter was talking with Jesus (1 John 21:15–17), after the resurrection? Jesus gave Peter three chances to say 'I love You' and after each of these chances, Jesus 're-branded' Peter: he was no longer the one who had rejected Jesus, instead he was a shepherd, a leader, a pastor of the early Church. Three times Peter said, 'I love You, Lord' but the really interesting thing is that the word Peter used for 'love' was not *agape* – the unconditional, all-consuming, never-ending powerful kind of love. No, it was *phileō* which means 'friendship love'. Peter said, three times, I 'friendship love' You. It was in response to Peter's friendship that Jesus called Peter to be a shepherd in the kingdom of God.

2. Revelation 19:7: 'Let us be glad and rejoice and give Him glory, for the marriage of the Lamb has come, and His wife has made herself ready.' Also Ephesians 5:25–27.

3. Youth With A Mission (YWAM) had a ship called M/V Pacific Link, then run by Marine Reach, a subdivision of YWAM. While I lived aboard, it was based in Tauranga, New Zealand.

4. The division of who is speaking to who is determined by the pronouns used in the original language (i.e. male, female, singular or plural). Mostly it is clear who is speaking but in a few verses, translations differ on who is speaking to whom in this book. I personally agree with J. Hudson Taylor's Commentary *Union and Communion*, first published before 1914, republished by Alpha International in June 2004. In Chapter 1:5 the Shulamite woman says 'I am dark' and the beloved replies 'but lovely'. The Shulamite woman then says 'dark like the [black] tents of Kedar' and the beloved replies 'like the [beautiful] tent curtains of Solomon'.

Chapter Fourteen

1. Gateway Church Audio Podcast 18.06.06.
2. Gary Chapman, *The Five Love Languages* (Chicago, IL: Moody Press, 2009)
3.http://www.fathers.com/documents/summit/Leadership%20Team%20Page/Father-Daughter%20Summit%20Introductory%20Presentation.pdf (accessed 6.12.16).
4. Linda Nielsen, PhD, professor of education and adolescent psychology at Wake Forest University quoted here: http://verilymag.com/2015/06/a-fathers-role-what-a-father-teaches-his-daughter-love-self-acceptance-healthy-relationships-dating-absent-fathers (accessed 7.12.16).
5. 'I Can Only Imagine' is written by Bart Millard, a member of the band MercyMe.
6. In the Old Testament, the Holy of Holies was the innermost room in the tabernacle (and later the temple) where the presence of God would descend. It could only be entered by certain people, wearing certain clothes, at certain times, after a ritual involving animal sacrifice, physical cleansing and prayer through the burning of incense (Exodus 40). The moment Jesus died on the cross, the extremely thick curtain to the Holy of Holies was torn from the top to bottom (Matthew 27:51). From this point on, the body of Christ collectively and Christians individually are called the temple of the Holy Spirit (Ephesians 2:19–22; 1 Corinthians 6:19). We have unhesitating access to God (Jesus was the sacrifice, His blood makes us clean and He is in the intercessor/intermediary for our prayers (Hebrews 10:19–22; 7:25).
7. Protection, provision, nurture/affection, training (as in, modelling lifestyle) and guidance (as in personal guidance).

Chapter Fifteen

1. J. Hudson Taylor, *Union and Communion: A Commentary on the Song of Songs* (London: Alpha International, 2004).

2. Dictionary.com Unabridged. Based on the Random House Dictionary, © Random House, Inc. 2016.
3. Matthew 5:5: 'Blessed are the meek, for they shall inherit the earth.'
4. Jeremiah 29:11: 'For I know the thoughts that I think toward you, says the LORD, thoughts of peace and not of evil, to give you a future and a hope.'
5. *The American Farmer,* Volume 40 (31 December 1819), digitalised by Google Commerce Ltd.
6. Ecclesiastes 4:12: 'a threefold cord is not quickly broken'.

Epilogue

1. Read this story in John 4.
2. John 4:23, NIV UK 2011.

Acknowledgements

A massive, heartfelt thank you...

...to God for saving me and giving me a testimony that has helped so many people already. To my dearest husband, Johnny, for such encouragement and support that I could never have dreamed possible. You are my gift from God and not a day goes by that I'm not thankful we are a part of each other's lives. I couldn't have written this book without your support and ever-constant love. To my daughters, who bring sunshine and joy into my life every single day. You are both so precious to me. To my ever-loving mum, for all your support and doing an outstanding job, bringing me up! To my generous dad, for rescuing me when I'm in trouble.

To Sharn Johnson, for being the best first-reviewer and encourager I could have asked for – this book would not have made it without you – God knew what He was doing the day He sent you to me. To Lucy – one of the first few to read a full draft – for giving me your time and encouragement as well as your powerful prayers.

For Cat Balo, Abigail Perano, Amy Wieman, Hayley Brewerton, Pastor Shane Jarvis and Pastors Mike and Amy de Vetter for asking me to share my story before I ever knew it mattered.

To Esther, Emma and Lisa for allowing me to share your lives with the world.

To the Oakes Gap Team Girls of 2014–15, who sacrificed their precious lunch hours to read and review each chapter, and pose for photos and vlogs – Becca Howe, Ciara Long, Erica Greaves, Dóra Budavári, Heidi Beatson, Becky Forrest, Fiona Houghton, Rebecca Mangles, Becca-Joy Martin, Erin Sorsbie, Bogi Szathmary, Sarah Udejiofo, Debs Lachlan and Renee Montaque.

And to Helen Windget, my most beautiful friend, for challenging me to realise that my wedding day was not the end of my story.

To Sarah Grace (Griggs) and Malcolm Down for believing in this book and persevering with me over many, many months in order that we might both – me and the book – reach our full potential. Thank you for helping me find the missing chapter. To Gareth Brocklebank for putting us in touch at just the right time – a truly God-made appointment happened there.

To Sammi Sparke, for stunning headshots.

And to my Y7 primary school teacher, Mr Bird: the first person to really believe in me.